T0345128

Mastering HTML

An open-source, HyperText Markup Language, or HTML is a programming language used in website building and website templates. It is used to format the look and format of a web page, to set design features such as basic layout, colors, and fonts. CSS allows for continuity between different web pages on the site and makes webpage development easier and faster. CSS frameworks are used for developing responsive and mobile-friendly websites.

Mastering HTML: A Beginner's Guide examines the fundamental concepts of HTML, its history, all the different versions available, and its advantages and disadvantages. Written in a concise and easy-to-understand format, each chapter includes examples and details of correct code output and HTML.

This book is a valuable resource for anyone who wants to create web page structures. After finishing this book, readers will be able to build their website quickly and with absolute ease.

Key Features:

- Discusses basic concepts of HTML such as common HTML attributes, doctype declaration, Block level elements, inline elements etc.

- Presents various elements, attributes and entities in HTML including a list of core attributes and entities used in HTML.

- Examines HTML Forms and other advanced topic such as Graphics, Canvas, SVG etc.

- Introduces text formatting and links tags used in HTML such as blockquote, quotation, anchor and many more.

About the Series

The Mastering Computer Science covers a wide range of topics, spanning programming languages as well as modern-day technologies and frameworks. The series has a special focus on beginner-level content, and is presented in an easy-to-understand manner, comprising:

- Crystal-clear text, spanning various topics sorted by relevance,
- Special focus on practical exercises, with numerous code samples and programs,
- A guided approach to programming, with step-by-step tutorials for the absolute beginners,
- Keen emphasis on real-world utility of skills, thereby cutting the redundant and seldom-used concepts and focusing instead of industry-prevalent coding paradigm,
- A wide range of references and resources, to help both beginner and intermediate-level developers gain the most out of the books.

Mastering Computer Science series of books start from the core concepts, and then quickly move on to industry-standard coding practices, to help learners gain efficient and crucial skills in as little time as possible. The books assume no prior knowledge of coding, so even the absolute newbie coders can benefit from this series.

Mastering Computer Science series is edited by Sufyan bin Uzayr, a writer and educator with over a decade of experience in the computing field.

For more information about this series, please visit: https://www.routledge.com/Mastering-Computer-Science/book-series/MCS

Mastering HTML
A Beginner's Guide

Edited by
Sufyan bin Uzayr

CRC Press is an imprint of the
Taylor & Francis Group, an **informa** business

First Edition published 2024
by CRC Press
2385 Executive Center Drive, Suite 320, Boca Raton, FL 33431

and by CRC Press
2 Park Square, Milton Park, Abingdon, Oxon, OX14 4RN

CRC Press is an imprint of Taylor & Francis Group, LLC

© 2024 Sufyan bin Uzayr

Library of Congress Cataloging-in-Publication Data

Names: Bin Uzayr, Sufyan, editor.
Title: Mastering HTML : a beginner's guide / edited by Sufyan bin Uzayr.
Description: First edition. | Boca Raton : CRC Press, 2023. | Series:
  Mastering computer science | Includes bibliographical references and
  index.
Identifiers: LCCN 2023003193 (print) | LCCN 2023003194 (ebook) | ISBN
  9781032414331 (paperback) | ISBN 9781032414362 (hardback) | ISBN
  9781003358077 (ebook)
Subjects: LCSH: HTML (Document markup language)--Amateurs' manuals.
Classification: LCC QA76.76.H94 M284 2023 (print) | LCC QA76.76.H94
  (ebook) | DDC 006.7/4--dc23/eng/20230414
LC record available at https://lccn.loc.gov/2023003193
LC ebook record available at https://lccn.loc.gov/2023003194

ISBN: 9781032414362 (hbk)
ISBN: 9781032414331 (pbk)
ISBN: 9781003358077 (ebk)

DOI: 10.1201/9781003358077

Typeset in Minion
by KnowledgeWorks Global Ltd.

For Mom

———————————

Contents

About the Editor

Sufyan bin Uzayr is a writer, coder, and entrepreneur with more than a decade of experience in the industry. He has authored several books in the past, pertaining to a diverse range of topics, ranging from History to Computers/IT.

Sufyan is the Director of Parakozm, a multinational IT company specializing in EdTech solutions. He also runs Zeba Academy, an online learning and teaching vertical with a focus on STEM fields.

Sufyan specializes in a wide variety of technologies such as JavaScript, Dart, WordPress, Drupal, Linux, and Python. He holds multiple degrees, including ones in Management, IT, Literature, and Political Science.

Sufyan is a digital nomad, dividing his time between four countries. He has lived and taught in numerous universities and educational institutions around the globe. Sufyan takes a keen interest in technology, politics, literature, history, and sports, and in his spare time, he enjoys teaching coding and English to young students.

Acknowledgments

There are many people who deserve to be on this page, for this book would not have come into existence without their support. That said, some names deserve a special mention, and I am genuinely grateful to:

- My parents, for everything they have done for me.

- The Parakozm team, especially Divya Sachdeva, Jaskiran Kaur, and Simran Rao, for offering great amounts of help and assistance during the book-writing process.

- The CRC team, especially Sean Connelly and Danielle Zarfati, for ensuring that the book's content, layout, formatting, and everything else remain perfect throughout.

- Reviewers of this book, for going through the manuscript and providing their insight and feedback.

- Typesetters, cover designers, printers, and everyone else, for their part in the development of this book.

- All the folks associated with Zeba Academy, either directly or indirectly, for their help and support.

- The programming community in general, and the web development community in particular, for all their hard work and efforts.

Sufyan bin Uzayr

Zeba Academy – Mastering Computer Science

The "Mastering Computer Science" series of books are authored by the Zeba Academy team members, led by Sufyan bin Uzayr, consisting of:

- Divya Sachdeva

- Jaskiran Kaur

- Simran Rao

- Aruqqa Khateib

- Suleymen Fez

- Ibbi Yasmin

- Alexander Izbassar

Zeba Academy is an EdTech venture that develops courses and content for learners primarily in STEM fields, and offers educational consulting and mentorship to learners and educators worldwide.

Additionally, Zeba Academy is actively engaged in running IT Schools in the CIS countries, and is currently working in partnership with numerous universities and institutions.

For more info, please visit https://zeba.academy

CHAPTER 1

Fundamentals of HTML

IN THIS CHAPTER

> ➤ Introduction

> ➤ History

> ➤ Structure of HTML

This HyperText Markup Language (HTML) book is for complete beginners, so it is written in a simple way so that the beginners do not get confused. For each theme and concept, we have provided an example with proper details of correct code output and legitimate HTML.

By the end of this HTML book, we're sure you'll be good at HTML and start creating your own web page structures. For this, you need to learn a few other technologies like Cascading Style Sheet (CSS) and JavaScript to create attractive and beautiful websites.

INTRODUCTION

HTML is a standard markup language for documents intended to be displayed in a web browser.[1] Technologies such as CSS and scripting languages such as JavaScript can help.

Web browsers receive various documents from a web server or local storage and convert them into multimedia web pages. HTML semantically defines the structure of a web page that originally contained guidelines for the appearance of a document.

DOI: 10.1201/9781003358077-1

HTML elements are the building blocks of HTML pages. HTML constructs can be used to insert images and other objects, such as interactive forms, into a rendered page. HTML provides a method for creating structured documents by marking the structural semantics of text, such as headings, paragraphs, lists, links, citations, and other items. HTML elements are separated by tags written using angular brackets. Tags like <img/> and <input/> directly insert content into the page. Other tags, such as <p>, provide information about the text of the document and can contain other tags as sub-elements. Browsers do not display HTML tags but use them to interpret page content.

Hypertext is text displayed on a system or other electronic device with links to other text that the user can access immediately, usually by clicking a mouse or pressing a key. In addition to text, hypertext can contain tables, lists, forms, images, and other presentation elements. It is an easy-to-use and flexible format for sharing information over the Internet.

Markup is the use of sets of markup tags to characterize textual elements in a document and give instructions to web browsers about how the document should look. HTML was originally developed by designers Tim Berners-Lee in 1990. He is known as the father of the web. But in 1996, the World Wide Web Consortium (W3C) became the authority for managing HTML specifications. HTML became an international standard (ISO) in 2000. Now, HTML5 is the new version of HTML. It provides a faster and more robust approach to web development.

HTML can embed programs written in different scripting languages, such as JavaScript, which affect the behavior and content of a web page; embedded elements define the appearance and layout of the content. The W3C, the former maintainer of HTML and the current maintainer of CSS standards, has supported the use of CSS over explicit presentational HTML since 1997. A form of HTML, known as the HTML5 version, is used to display video and audio using the <canvas> element in connection with JavaScript.

A BRIEF HISTORY OF HTML

In 1993, the first version was written by Tim Berners-Lee. Since then, there have been many various versions of HTML.[2] The most widely used version was the 2000s was HTML 4, which became an official standard in December 1999.

Another version, XHTML, was a rewrite version of HTML as XML. It is a standard markup language that is used to create other markup languages. Hundreds of XML languages are included like GML, MathML, MusicML, and RSS. Because each of these languages was written in a common language (XML), their content can be easily shared between applications. It makes XML potentially very powerful, and it's no surprise that the W3C created an XML version of HTML again called XHTML. It became an official standard in 2000 and was updated in 2002. It is very similar to HTML but with some stricter rules. Sometimes strict rules are necessary for all XML languages because without them interoperability between applications would not be possible.

Most pages on the Web were built using either 4.01 or XHTML 1.0. However, in recent years, the W3C has been working on a new version of HTML, i.e. HTML5. It is still a draft specification not yet an official standard. However, it is widely supported by browsers and other web-enabled devices.

The following lists the many types of content that can add to web pages using other versions of HTML. In the early days, HTML was so simple, but over time new versions were released that added more and more features. However, if web designers wanted to add content or functionality that HTML did not support, they would have to do so using nonstandard proprietary technologies such as Adobe. These technologies require users to install browser plug-ins and in some cases would mean that some users are not able to access the content. HTML5 added support for many new features that will allow you to do more with HTML without relying on nonstandard proprietary technologies.

Type of HTML Content	HTML 1.2	HTML 4.01	HTML5	Purpose
Heading	Yes	Yes	Yes	It is used to organize page content by adding headings and subheadings to the top of each section of the page
Paragraph	Yes	Yes	Yes	It identifies the paragraphs of text
Address that contains contact information	Yes	Yes	Yes	It identifies a block of text

(Continued)

Type of HTML Content	HTML 1.2	HTML 4.01	HTML5	Purpose
Anchor	Yes	Yes	Yes	It links to other web content
List	Yes	Yes	Yes	It organizes items into a list
Image	Yes	Yes	Yes	It is used to embed a photograph or drawing into a web page
Table	No	Yes	Yes	It organizes data into rows and columns
Style	No	Yes	Yes	It adds CSS to control how objects on a web page are presented
Script	No	Yes	Yes	It adds Javascript to make pages respond to user behaviors (more interactive)
Audio	No	No	Yes	It adds audio to a web page with a single tag
Video	No	No	Yes	It adds video to a web page with a single tag
Canvas	No	No	Yes	It adds an invisible drawing pad to a web page, on which you can add drawings using Javascript

The first description of HTML was "HTML Tags", first mentioned on the Internet by Tim Berners-Lee in late 1991.[3] It describes the 18 elements that make up the initial, relatively simple HTML design. Apart from the hyperlink tag, these were heavily influenced by SGMLguid, an internal documentation format based on the Standard Generalized Markup Language (SGML) at CERN. Eleven of these elements still exist in HTML 4.

HTML is a markup language that browsers use to compose text, images, and other material into visual or audio web pages. The default properties for each HTML tag item are defined in the browser, and these properties can be changed or enhanced by further use of the website designer's CSS.

Many text elements are found in the 1988 technical report ISO TR 9537 Techniques for use of SGML, which in turn covers features of early text formatting languages, such as the language used by the RUNOFF command, which was developed in the early 1960s for Compatible

Time-Sharing System (CTSS) operating system and these formatting commands were derived from commands used by compositors to manually format documents.

However, SGML is the concept of generalized markup that is based on elements (nested annotated scopes with attributes) rather than just print effects, with structure and markup also separated; HTML gradually moved in this direction with CSS.

WHY HTML IS CALLED A MARKUP LANGUAGE?

HTML is called a markup language. It defines the structure and layout of the content that users can see on a web page.[4] HTML is the most popular markup language in the world; more than 94% of websites use HTML as their markup language. It uses tags and various attributes to format the text you see when you visit a web page and describes how to display content.

The latest version of HTML5 is now widely adopted by developers and is used on around 90% of websites. Don't get confused by these two terms, HTML and HTML5. They are the same, but HTML introduced newer features to the most popular markup language.

Let's have a look at what a markup language is and why it is considered a markup language. We will then explore other markup languages available to software engineers today.

WHAT IS A MARKUP LANGUAGE?

A markup language is a basically coding system that is included in text documents to structure, format, and display various elements on a page. It is interpreted by various devices, such as your Internet browser, and controls how the document is displayed or printed. The markup languages contain two main data types such as the text that will be displayed, and then the markup describing how to display it. It means structuring in a specific way. So the markup language explains to your browser how the document should be laid out. CSS is a style sheet language that is paired with markup languages such as HTML to improve the appearance of markup. Users do not see markup languages when viewing a web page or document. It is interpreted by a device that only displays the actual text you want the audience to see.

Markup languages are essential for accessibility. These languages allow screen readers and other browsing aids to see what the user is looking at. HTML is a markup language because it defines the structure, as well as format and layout of the content we want to display on a web page. It lets any browser know how you want your website content to appear. More than 90% of websites use HTML5, making it the most popular markup language in the world.

HTML actually stands for Hypertext Markup Language. Hypertext refers to the fact that it is machine-readable, while markup language indicates that it is used for structuring and organization. It is a set of rules that grow the appearance of pages on the Internet and how they connect to the rest of the Web.

When we create HTML pages, the markup is never displayed to the user. Open the webpage and you will see the relevant text, images, and videos. However, HTML is pulling the strings behind all of this. It lets any browser know how you want things organized. HTML allows you to group paragraphs, headings, images, videos, and more. It allows to create complex forms and displays information exactly the way you want.

An often overlooked feature of HTML as a markup language is how it links pages together. It is important for search engines and users to know which pages are relevant to each other and how you want to link them. Without HTML, users wouldn't be able to navigate your site or visit the links you recommend. Remember that a markup document has two types of content.

HTML is not the markup language; however, it is the most well-known, as 94% of websites use it as a markup language. Its ease of use made it the markup language of the web, but there are various markup languages out there, all with a variety of different uses.

HTML is generally much more forgiving than other markup languages such as XML. It is case insensitive and will compile even if you omit the closing tag. HTML is easy to use the starting point for people learning web development for decades. It pairs well with CSS and frameworks like Bootstrap. As we mentioned earlier, markup languages define the way electronic documents are interpreted. They specify how something is displayed or what they mean. It is not the only markup language, other markup languages include:

1. EBM

2. GML

3. SGML

4. XML

5. YAML

6. GLML

7. HTML

8. KML

9. MathML

10. SGML

11. TIME

12. EMAIL

13. VTML

14. XHTML

DIFFERENT VERSIONS OF HTML

HTML has never been the way it is right now.[5] HTML, like many other languages, has evolved over time and is much better and more versatile today than it was a long time ago. Different versions of HTML have different properties. But today we use HTML5, which is the latest version of HTML.

- HTML 1.0 (released in 1991)
- HTML 2.0 (released in 1995)
- HTML 3.2 (released in 1997)
- HTML 4.01 (released in 1999)
- XHTML (released in 2000)
- HTML5 (released in 2014)

HTML 1.0

It was the basic version of HTML with less support for a wide range of HTML elements. It does not have rich features such as styling and other things that related to how content will be rendered in a browser. This initial version doesn't provide support for tables, font support, etc.

HTML 2

It was developed in 1995 to improve HTML version 1.0. It was developed to maintain common rules and regulations across different browsers. It improves a lot in terms of marker marks. In version 2.0, the concept of form came into effect. Forms were developed but still had basic markup like text boxes, buttons, etc.

Also, the table came as an HTML tag. Now, in version 2.0, browsers also came up with the concept of creating custom markup layers that were specific to the browser itself. The main intention of the W3C is to maintain standards across different web browsers so that those browsers understand and render HTML tags in a similar way.

HTML 3.2

HTML 3.2 was published by W3C Recommendation. It was the very first version developed exclusively by the W3C. With HTML 3.2, HTML tags were further improved. It had many new features like tables, superscript, subscript, etc. The two most important features introduced in it were tables and text flow around images.

Now has better support for new form elements. Another important feature it implemented was CSS support. It is CSS that provides functions that will make HTML tags look better when rendered in browsers. CSS helps style HTML elements.

After browsers were upgraded to it, the browser also supported frame tags, although the HTML specification still does not support iframe tags. Tables were widely used and are still used by programmers, but it is no longer recommended. In HTML5, div tags and other semantic elements are more often used instead of the table element.

HTML 4.01

It is the expanded support for CSSs. In version 3.2, CSS was embedded into the HTML page itself. So if a website has different web pages to apply the style of each page, we need to put CSS on each web page. So there was a repetition of the same CSS block.

To overcome this, the concept of an external style sheet appeared in version 4.01. Under this concept, an external CSS file could be developed and this external style file could be included in the HTML itself. HTML 4.01 provided support for additional new HTML tags.

HTML 4.01 was a revised version of HTML 4.0; it also included features for people with disabilities to improve their interactivity with the global world through the Internet.

XHTML

XHTML called as Extensible HTML.[6] It can consider as a part of the XML markup language because it has features of both XML and HTML. It is the extended form of XML and HTML. It can also be considered as a better version of HTML.

XHTML version:

- XHTML is a different language that began as a reformulation of HTML 4.01 using XML 1.0. Now, it is no longer being developed as a stand-alone standard.

- XHTML version 1.0 was published as a W3C Recommendation on January 26, 2000, and later revised and republished on August 1, 2002.

- XHTML 1.1 was published on May 31, 2001, as W3C Recommendation. It is based on the XHTML 1.0 Strict, but with minor changes, it can be adapted.

- XHTML 2.0 was abandoned in 2009 in favor of work on HTML5 and XHTML5. XHTML 2.0 was now incompatible with XHTML 1.x.

HTML5

HTML5 is the best version of HTML to date. HTML5 has improved user interactivity so much and also reduced the load on the device.

HTML5 fully supports all kinds of media applications out there. It supports both audio and video media content. It also provides full support for running JavaScript in the background.

MARKUP IN HTML

HTML markup consists of various key components, including those called tags (their attributes), character-based data types, character references, and entity references. HTML tags are most often found in pairs such as <h1> and </h1>, although some represent empty elements and are therefore unpaired, such as <img>. The first tag is a pair is the start tag, and the second is the end tag (also called opening tags and ending tags).

Another important part is the HTML document type declaration that triggers standard mode rendering.

The following is an example of the program given below.

```
<!DOCTYPE html>
<html>
  <head>
    <title> Document Title </title>
  </head>
  <body>
    <div>
        <p> You are learning HTML! </p>
    </div>
  </body>
</html>
```

The text between <html> – </html> describes the web page, the text between <body> and </body> is the visible content of the page. The <title>This is a title</title> tag defines the browser page title displayed on browser tabs and window titles, and the <div> tag defines page divisions used for easy styling. A <meta> element can be used between <head> and </head> to define a web page's metadata.

The <!DOCTYPE html> document type declaration is for HTML5. If the declaration is not included, various browsers fall back into "quirks mode" for rendering.

HTML DOCUMENT TYPE

All HTML documents must begin with a <!DOCTYPE> declaration. A declaration is not an HTML tag. It is "information" to the browser about what type of document to expect.

In HTML5, the <!DOCTYPE> declaration is simple. The <!DOCTYPE> declaration is NOT case-sensitive.

Examples:

- <!DOCTYPE html>

- <!DocType html>

- <!Doctype html>

- <!doctype html>

BASIC HTML CONCEPTS

There are some basic HTML concepts such as elements, tags, and attributes.[7] Elements are a main structural unit of a web page. The tags are used to define HTML elements, and attributes provide additional information about these elements.

HTML Tags

Basically, tags are used to structure website content (text, hyperlinks, images, media, etc.).[8] These are not displayed in browsers; they only "instruct" browsers how to display the content of the web page.

There are over hundreds of tags and you can find them in any other HTML lesson. These tags are written in curly brackets (e.g. <html>). Most HTML tags come in pairs, such as <p> </p> tags. The first tag in the pair is called the start (opening) tag and the second tag is the end (closing) tag. The information is written between the opening and closing tags. However, there are unpaired or empty tags that only have a start tag. (e.g. <img/>).

A document is created using different types of tags. HTML tags can be defined and divided on a different basis. Let's take a look at the following sections of this chapter. We have divided these tags based on the following classifications:

- Paired and Unpaired Tags

- Self-Closing Tags

- Utility-Based Tags

Let's explain the following are the paired and unpaired tags in HTML in detail with the help of examples.

Paired Tag

An open tag is known as a paired tag if the tag consists of a start tag and an end tag as a companion tag. An HTML Paired tag begins with an opening tag: the name of the tag enclosed in curly brackets; for example, the paragraph opening tag is written as "<p>". Content follows a start tag that ends with an end tag: tag name starting with a slash; for example, a paragraph end tag is written as "</p>". The first label can be labeled "Opening tag" and the second label can be called the "Closing tag".

Here is the list of some paired tags in HTML such as,

Open Tag	Close Tag
<div>	</div>
<table>	</table>
<form>	</form>
<span>	</span>
<p>	</p>
<ul>	</ul>
<html>	</html>
<head>	</head>

Unpaired Tags

An HTML tag is called an odd tag if the tag has only an opening tag and no closing tag or accompanying tag. The Unpaired tag does not require a closing tag; with this type, an opening label is sufficient. Unpaired tags are also sometimes named single tags or singular tags because they do not require any accompanying tag.

It is to close the unpaired/singular tags. But unfortunately, we do not have the closing tag. So, an unpaired tag is closed putting behind a slash(/) before the greater than > sign. For example: <bru/>. Now below is the list of some unpaired tags in HTML. The use of slash(/) in the tags is to close them. Here are some unpaired tags:

1. Open Tag:

   - <hr>

   - <meta>

2.
:

   - <input>

Heading Tags (H1 Tag to H6 Tag)

These are used to give headings of different sizes in a document. There are six different heading tags, which give various heading sizes and are defined by <h1> – <h6> tags. <h1> gives the biggest heading and <h6> gives the smallest one. So <h1> can be used for important headings for bold headings, and <h6> can be used for a least important ones.

```
<!DOCTYPE html>
<html lang="en">
<head>
 <meta charset="UTF-8">
 <title> HTML Heading Tag </title>
</head>
<body>
<h1> This is Heading 1 </h1>
 <h2> This is Heading 2 </h2>
<h3> This is Heading 3 </h3>
<h4> This is Heading 4 </h4>
<h5> This is Heading 5 </h5>
<h6> This is Heading 6 </h6>
</body>
</html>
```

HTML p Tag – Paragraph Tag

The <p> tag defines a paragraph in a document. An HTML paragraph or HTML <p> tag provides the text inside the paragraph as completion. It is noteworthy that the browser itself adds line breaks before and after the paragraph.

We'll show you how it works with a simple example.

```
<!DOCTYPE html>
<html lang="en">
<head>
 <meta charset="UTF-8">
 <title> HTML Paragraph Tag </title>
</head>
<body>
<p> This is First Paragraph </p>
 <p> This is Second Paragraph </p>
<p> This is Third Paragraph </p>
</body>
</html>
```

HTML Tag – Anchor Tag

An HTML hyperlink is defined using the <a> tag (Anchor tag). It is used to create a link to any file, web page, image, etc.

This tag is called an anchor tag, and anything between the opening <a> tag and closing </a> tag is a part of the link, and the user can click on that part to go to the linked document.

```
<!DOCTYPE html>
<HTML lang="en">
<head>
 <meta charset="UTF-8">
 <title> Anchor Tag </title>
</head>
<body>
<a target="_blank" href="https://www.google.com">
This is a link </a>
</body>
</html>
```

HTML img Tag– Image Tag

The image is used to add images to HTML documents.[9] The img tag is used to add an image to a document. The 'src' is used to specify the source of the image. The height and width of the image can control the – height="px" and width="px".

The alt is used as an alternative if the image is not displayed. Whatever is written as the value of this attribute is displayed. It provides information about the image.

```
<!DOCTYPE html>
<html lang="en">
<head>
  <meta charset="UTF-8">
  <title> Image Tag </title>
</head>
<body>
<img src=image-1.png" width="400px" height="200px">
</body>
</html>
```

Self-Closing Tags

Self-closing tags are HTML tags that do not have a partner tag, where the first tag is the only tag needed that is valid for formatting. The main and important information is contained INSIDE the element as its attribute. An "img" tag is a simple example of a self-closing tag. Let's see it in action below.

```
<!DOCTYPE html>
<html lang="en">
<head>
  <meta charset="UTF-8">
  <title> HTML Image Tag </title>
</head>
<body>
<img src="image-1.png" width="400px" height="200px">
</body>
</html>
```

Utility-Based Tags

HTML tags can be broadly differentiated based on their usefulness, i.e. based on the purpose they serve. We can basically divide them into three categories as below:

- Formatting tags
- Structure marks
- Control labels

HTML tags that help us in formatting texts like text size, font styles, making text bold, etc. This is done using <font>, <b>, <u>, etc. tags. Tables Tags, divisions, and span are also those tags that help to format a web page or document and set the page layout. Below is a small program that uses a break to format a page along with some other formatting tags.

```
<html>
<head>
<title> Title </title>
</head>
<body>
```

```
<div class="container">
<div class="row">
<div class="col-25">
<label for="email"> <b>Name</b> </label>
</div>
<div class="col-35">
<input type="text" placeholder="First Name"
name="fname" required>
</div>
<div class="col-35">
<input type="text" placeholder="Last Name"
name="lname" required>
</div>
</div>
</div>
</body>
</html>
```

Structure Tags

HTML tags that help structure an HTML document are called Structure Tags. Description, title, HTML, heading, body, etc. form a group of page structure tags. Structure tags only help in building or creating a basic HTML page from the root; that is, they do not affect or participate in text formatting. The basic HTML program is therefore a basic group of structural tags.

```
<!doctype html>
<html>
<head>
<meta charset="utf-8">
<title>Types of Tags Demo</title>
</head>
<body>
<p> This is a paragraph </p>
<i><b> This is a bold and italicized text </b></i>
</body>
</html>
```

Control Tags

Another category of tags that can be created is 'Control Tags'. Script tags, radio buttons or checkboxes, Form tags, etc. are control tags. These are tags that are used when managing content or managing scripts or libraries that are external. All form tags, drop-downs, input text fields, etc. are used when interacting with a visitor or user.

The HTML tags are based on the type of tags and their usefulness. HTML tags can also be easily divided based on basic categories such as basic HTML root tags, formatting tags, audio and video tags, form and input tags, frames, links, lists, tables, styles, meta tags, etc.

HTML Tag List

There are various tags in HTML. You will get tags in alphabetical order below.[10]

Tags	Description
<!--...-->	It describes a comment text in the source code
<!doctype>	It defines a document type
<a>	It specifies an anchor (Hyperlink)
	It is used for link in internal/external web documents
<abbr>	It describes an abbreviation (acronyms)
<acronym>	It describes an acronyms
<address>	It describes an address information
<applet>	It describes embedding an applet in HTML document
<area>	It defines an area in an image map
<article>	It defines an article
<aside>	It describes contain set
<audio>	It specifies audio content
<b>	It specifies text weight bold
<base>	It define a base URL for all the links within a web page
<basefont>	It describes a default font color, size, and face in a document
<bb>	It defines browser command that invokes as per client action
<bdo>	It specifies direction of text display
<big>	It defines a big text
<blockquote>	It specifies a long quotation
<body>	It specifies a main section(body) part in HTML document
 	It specifies a single line break
<button>	It specifies a press/push button
<canvas>	It specifies the display graphics on HTML web document
<caption>	It specifies a table caption
<center>	It specifies a text is display in center align
<cite>	It specifies a text citation
<code>	It specifies computer code text
<col>	It specifies a column within a <colgroup> element in table
<colgroup>	It specifies a group of more columns inside table
<command>	It specifies a command button that invokes as per user action

(Continued)

Tags	Description
<datagrid>	It specifies a represent data in Datagrid either list wise or tree wise
<datalist>	It specifies a list of predefined options for an <input> element that used to provide an "autocomplete" feature for <input> elements. The <datalist> element's id attribute must be equal to the <input> element's list attribute
<dd>	It specifies a definition description in a definition list
<del>	It specifies text deleted in web document
<details>	It specifies an additional details hide or show as per user action
<dfn>	It specifies a definition team
<dialog>	It specifies a chat conversation between one and more person
<dir>	It specifies a directory list
<div>	It specifies a division part
<dl>	It specifies a definition list
<dt>	It specifies a definition team
<em>	It specifies a text that is in emphasized format.
<embed>	It defines an embedding external application using a relative plug-in
<eventsource>	It defines a source of event that generates to remote server
<fieldset>	It defines a grouping of related form elements
<figcaption>	It defines a caption text corresponding with a figure element
<figure>	It defines self-contained content corresponding with a <figcaption> element
<font>	It defines a font size, font face, and font color for its text
<footer>	It defines a footer section containing details about the author, copyright, contact us, sitemap, or links to related documents
<frame>	It defines frame window
<frameset>	It is used to hold one or more <frame> elements
<form>	It defines a form section that has interactive input controls to submit form information to a server
<h1> to <h6>	It defines a Headings level from 1 to 6 of different sizes
<head>	It defines header section of HTML document.
<header>	It defines as a container that holds introductory content or navigation links
<hgroup>	It describes the heading of a section that holds the h1 to h6 tags <hr /> It represents a thematic break between paragraph-level tags. It typically draws horizontal line
<html>	It defines a document as an HTML markup language
<i>	It defines an italic format text
<iframe>	It defines an inline frame that embedded external content into current web document
<img>	It is used to insert image into a web document
<input>	It defines a get information in the selected input
<ins>	It is used to indicate text that is inserted into a page and indicates changes to a document
<isindex>	It is used to create a single-line search prompt for querying the contents of the document

(Continued)

Tags	Description
<kbd>	It is used to identify text that represents keyboard input
<keygen>	It is used to generate a signed certificate, which is used to authenticate services
<label>	It is used to caption a text label with a form <input> element
<legend>	It is used to add a caption (title) to a group of related form elements that are joined together into the <fieldset> tag
<li>	It defines a list item either an ordered list or an unordered list
<link>	It is used to load external style sheets into HTML document
<map>	It defines a clickable image map
<mark>	It is used to highlight (marked) specific text
<menu>	It is used to display an unordered list of items/menu of commands
<meta>	It is used to provide structured metadata about a web page
<meter>	It is used to measure data within a given range
<nav>	It is used to define a group of navigation links
<noframes>	It used to provide a fallback content to the browser that does not support the <frame> element
<noscript>	It is used to provide a fall-back content to the browser that does not support the JavaScript
<object>	It is used to embed objects such as images, audio, videos, Java applets, and Flash animations
<ol>	It defines an ordered list of items
<optgroup>	It is used to create a grouping of options; the related options are grouped under specific headings
<option>	It represents option items within a <select>, <optgroup>, or <datalist> element
<output>	It is used for representing the result of a calculation
<p>	It is used to represent a paragraph of text
<param>	It provides parameters for embedded object element
<pre>	It is used to represent preformatted text
<progress>	It represents the progress of a task
<q>	It represents the short quotation
<rp>	It is used to provide parentheses around fall-back content to the browser that does not support the ruby annotations
<rt>	It specifies the ruby text of ruby annotation
<ruby>	It is used to represent a ruby annotation
<s>	The text displays in strikethrough style
<samp>	It represents text that should be interpreted as sample output from a computer program
<script>	It defines client-side JavaScript
<section>	It is used to divide a document into a number of different generic sections
<select>	It is used to create a drop-down list
<small>	It is used to make the text one size smaller
<source>	It is used to specify multiple media resources
<span>	It is used to group and apply styles to inline elements

(Continued)

Tags	Description
<strike>	It represents strikethrough text.
<strong>	It represents strong emphasis greater important text
<style>	It is used to add CSS style to an HTML document
<sub>	It represents inline subscript text
<sup>	It defines inline superscript text
<table>	It is used to define a table in an HTML document
<tbody>	It is used for grouping table rows.
<td>	It is used for creates standard data cell in an HTML table
<textarea>	It creates multi-line text input
<tfoot>	It is used to add a footer to a table that contains a summary of the table data
<th>	It is used to create header of a group of cells in an HTML table
<thead>	It is used to add a header to a table that contains header information of the table
<time>	It represents the date and/or time in an HTML document
<title>	It represents title to an HTML document
<tr>	It represents a row of cells in a table
<track>	It defines text tracks for both <audio> and <video> tags
<tt>	It defines teletype text
<u>	It defines underlined text
<ul>	It defines an unordered list of items
<var>	It defines a variable in a computer program or mathematical equation
<video>	Used to embed video content
<wbr>	It defines a word break opportunity in a long word

STRUCTURE OF AN HTML DOCUMENT

The <!DOCTYPE html> declaration specifies the version of HTML used in the document.[11] Every HTML document must start with this declaration so that browsers can render the page in accordance with HTML standards.

There are several <!DOCTYPE> types defined for each version of HTML. <!DOCTYPE> – The doctype declaration indicates the type of document and version of HTML used on the web page. Each version has a different doctype declaration. This example uses the HTML5 Doctype.

```
<!DOCTYPE>
```

All content on a web page is written between <html> and </html> tags. The <html> element is used to tell browsers that this is an HTML document. <html> – It is the root tag of the document that describes the entire web page. It is also paired tag, i.e. it also has a closing </html> tag. Everything will be written inside these tags.

```
<html>
//rest of the code
</html>
```

The <head> element contains metadata (that is data about the HTML document), character set, document name, styles, etc. This data is not displayed to viewers. This tag contains information about the document, such as its title, author information, web page description, and so on. It has various tags to perform these functions. It is also a couple tag.

```
<head>
 . . rest of the code
 </head>
```

The <title> shows the title of the website in the browser tab when the page is loaded. It is written between <title> and </title> tags.

```
<title>
 . . rest of the code
 </title>
```

The <body> tag contains the content of the web page (i.e. text, images, videos, etc.). Content is written between <body> and </body>. The body tag contains every information that will be displayed on the web page. If you want anything to appear on the page, you must write it in these tags.

```
<body>
 . . rest of the code
</body>
```

Heading elements contain different types of headings. There are six heading levels – <h1> – <h6>, where <h1> is the most important and <h6> least important tags.

```
<h1> </h1>
<h2> </h2>
<h3> </h3>
<h4> </h4>
```

```
<h5> </h5>
<h6> </h6>
```

The <p> element contains paragraphs of the text. The content is written between <p> and </p> tags.

```
<p> </p>
```

Example:

```
<!DOCTYPE HTML>
<html>
  <head>
    <meta HTTP-equiv="Content-Type" content="text/
HTML; charset=utf-8">
    <title>Title of the document</title>
    <style>
    body{
      width:500px;
      margin:0 auto,
    }
    </style>
  </head>

  <body>
    <h1>
      Structure of an HTML Document
    </h1>
    <h2> Aenean placerat commodo tortor at ornare.
Suspendisse et rutrum eros. In quis velit nunc.
Fusce auctor felis id tellus euismod aliquam.
Pellentesque habitant morbi senectus et netus et
malesuada fames ac turpis egestas.
    </h2>
      <p>Donec vitae pharetra nisl. Nulla consequat,
purus semper viverra congue, risus ex bibendum
urna, nec fringilla mi ipsum in mauris. Curabitur
id bibendum arcu, id efficitur risus. </p>
      <h2> Nulla consequat, purus semper viverra
congue, risus ex bibendum urna, nec  </h2>
  </body>
</html>
```

HTML EDITORS AND TOOLS

If you've heard of web development, the term HTML should sound familiar.[12] HTML is one of the most important and common elements that define the structure of the web.

The most common functions in a good HTML editor are:

- It can be used to distinguish HTML tags in different colors based on the categories, making it easier to read and recognize the structure of the code.

- The automatic suggestion of HTML elements and attributes based on previously added values, time-saving when typing a longer piece of code.

- It can easily scan for syntax errors whenever you type in code incorrectly to fix the mistake immediately and make them highlight.

- It helps to find out particular code and replace them all at once, saving time from editing each string of code.

- It connects web server with an FTP client right from the dashboard.

- It can hide a section of code and focuses on certain parts of the HTML document.

WHAT IS AN HTML EDITOR?

An editor is software for creating and editing HTML code.[13] It can be standalone software designed for writing and editing code or part of an Integrated Development Environment (IDE). The HTML editor provides more advanced features and is specially designed for developers to create websites more efficiently. It ensures that every line of code is clean and working properly.

There are several professional editors that web developers use for coding. However, not every editor can satisfy all your needs. A good HTML editor must therefore have the following features:

- syntax highlighting – display of text, especially source code, in different colors and fonts,

- tab display support – keep multiple web pages open in tabs at the same time,

- checking for errors in the HTML document, and

- code wrapping – hiding large code fragments leaving only a line.

Some HTML editors can also translate HTML into a programming language such as CSS, XML, or JavaScript. This means that different types of HTML editors can offer different sets of functions and features.

The most popular HTML editors are listed below:

- WebStorm

- Visual Studio Code

- Atom

- Sublime text

- Notepad++

- HTML-Kit

- CoffeeCup

- Notepad++

- Bluefish

- Sublime

HTML ELEMENT SYNTAX

An HTML element is a separate part of an HTML document. It represents semantics or meaning. For example, the title element defines the title of the document.

Most HTML elements start with a start tag (or opening tag) and an end tag (or closing tag), with content in between. The elements can also contain attributes that define their other properties.

HTML uses tags for its syntax. The tag consists of special characters: <, >, and /. They are interpreted by software to create an HTML element.

```
<p class="text"> This is a paragraph </p>
```

CASE INSENSITIVITY IN TAGS AND ATTRIBUTES

There are some tag and attribute names that are not case-sensitive (but most attribute values are case-sensitive). It means the tag <p> is the same as tag <P>. In XHTML, they are case-sensitive and the tag <P> is different from the tag <p>.

Example:

```
<!DOCTYPE HTML>
<html>
  <head>
    <meta HTTP-equiv="Content-Type" content="text/
HTML; charset=utf-8">
    <title>Title of the document</title>
    <style>
    body{
      width:500px;
      margin:0 auto,
    }
    </style>
  </head>

  <body>
    <h1> Case Insensitivity in Tags and Attributes
</h1>
    <p> This is a paragraph. </p>
<P> This is also paragraph. </P>
  </body>
</html>
```

EMPTY HTML ELEMENTS

Empty elements (also called self-closing, void elements) are not container tags, you cannot write <hr> here is your some content</hr> or
some content</br>. A common example is the <br> element, which represents a line break. Some other common empty elements are <img>, <meta>, <input>, <link>, <hr>, etc.

Example:

```
<p>This paragraph contains break tag <br> that
break line. </p>
```

```
<img src="images-1.jpg" alt=" Keyword of image ">
<input type="text" name="user_name">
```

NESTING HTML ELEMENTS

Most HTML elements can contain a number of further elements, which are made up of tags, attributes, and content or other elements.

Example:

```
<!DOCTYPE HTML>
<html>
  <head>
    <meta content="text/HTML; HTTP-equiv="Content-
Type" charset=utf-8">
    <title>Title of the document</title>
    <style>
    Body {
      width:500px;
      margin:0 auto,
    }
    </style>
  </head>

  <body>
    <h1> Nesting HTML Elements </h1>
    p> This is a paragraph that contain <b>bold</b>
text.</p>
    <p>This is a paragraph that contain  <em>
emphasized </em> text. </p>
    <p>This is a paragraph that contain  <mark>
highlighted </mark> text. </p>

</html>
```

HTML COMMENTS

The comments are usually added with the purpose of making the source code easier to understand. It may help other developers to understand what you were trying to do with the HTML. Comments are not displayed in the browser.

Syntax:

```
<!-- Comments here -->
```

An HTML comment starts with <!-- and ends with --> as shown in the example below.

```
<!-- This is an HTML comment -->
<!-- This is a multiline HTML comment
     which includes more than one line --> '
     <p>This is a normal text.</p>
```

The comment tag is useful when debugging code.

- This is a simple piece of code that web browsers delete (ignore), i.e. the browser does not display it.

- It helps the coder and the reader to understand the part of code used especially in complex source code.

TYPES OF HTML COMMENTS

There are three types of comments in HTML given below:

- Single line comment: A single line comment is given inside a tag (<!– comment –>).

- Multi-line comment: Multi-line comment can be given by the syntax (<!– –>), basically it is the same as used in single line comment, the difference is half of the comment part (" –> ") is appended where to intended the comment line ends.

- Using the <comment> tag: There used to be an HTML <comment> tag, but it is currently not supported by any modern browser.

Importance:

- It improves code readability, especially when multiple developers access a single HTML document.

- It ensures fast and efficient understanding of complex codes.

- It makes debugging the source code easier and makes it easier to maintain.

TYPES OF HTML ELEMENTS

Elements can be placed in two different groups such as block-level elements and row-level elements. The former forms the structure of the document, while the latter dresses the contents of the block.

The block element also takes up 100% of the available width and is rendered with line breaks before and after. Whereas an inline element only takes up as much space as it needs.

The most commonly used block level elements are <div>, <p>, <h1> to <h6>, <form>, <ol>, <ul>, <li>, etc. While the commonly used row-level elements are <img >, <a>, <span>, <strong>, <b>, <em>, <i>, <code>, <input>, <button>, etc.

HTML ATTRIBUTES

It defines other characteristics or properties of the element, such as the width and height of the image.[14] Attributes are always specified in the opening tag and consist of name/value pairs like name="value". Attribute values always are enclosed in quotation marks.

Some attributes are also required for certain elements. For example, the <img> tag must contain the src and alt attributes. Let's look at some examples of using attributes.

```
<!DOCTYPE html>
<html lang="en">
<head>
    <meta charset="UTF-8">
    <meta HTTP-equiv="X-UA-Compatible"
content="IE=edge">
    <meta name="viewport" content="width=device-width,
initial-scale=1.0">
    <title>Document</title>
</head>
<body>
    <img src="images/ball.png" width="30" height="30"
alt="Smiley">
<a href="https://www.google.com" title="Search
Engine">Google</a>
<abbr title="Hyper Text Markup Language">HTML</abbr>
<input type="text" value="John Doe">
</body>
</html>
```

There are several other attributes that do not consist of name/value pairs but consist of just name. These attributes are called Boolean attributes. Examples of some used Boolean attributes are such as checked, disabled, readonly, required, etc.

Example:

```
<!DOCTYPE html>
<html lang="en">
<head>
    <meta charset="UTF-8">
    <meta HTTP-equiv="X-UA-Compatible"
content="IE=edge">
    <meta name="viewport" content="width=device-
width, initial-scale=1.0">
    <title>Document</title>
</head>
<body>
    <input type="email" required>
    <input type="submit" value="Submit" disabled>
    <input type="checkbox" checked>
    <input type="text" value="Read_only_text"
readonly>
</body>
</html>
```

GENERAL ATTRIBUTES

There are some attributes, such as id, style, title, class, etc., that you can use on the majority of HTML elements.[15] The following sections describe their usage.

The id Attribute

It is used to give a unique name or identifier to an element within a document. It makes it easier to select the element using CSS or JavaScript.

```
<!DOCTYPE html>
<html lang="en">
<head>
    <meta charset="UTF-8">
    <meta HTTP-equiv="X-UA-Compatible"
content="IE=edge">
```

```
    <meta name="viewport" content="width=device-width,
initial-scale=1.0">
    <title>Document</title>
</head>
<body>
    <input type="text" id="firstName">
    <div id="container">Some content</div>
    <p id="info text">This is a paragraph.</p>
</body>
</html>
```

The class Attribute

Same as id attribute, the class attribute is also used to identify elements. But unlike id, the class attribute doesn't have to be unique in the HTML document. It means you can apply the same class to multiple elements in a document, as shown in the following example.

```
<!DOCTYPE html>
<html lang="en">
<head>
    <meta charset="UTF-8">
    <meta HTTP-equiv="X-UA-Compatible"
content="IE=edge">
    <meta name="viewport" content="width=device-width,
initial-scale=1.0">
    <title>Document</title>
</head>
<body>
    <input type="text" class="highlight">
    <div class="box highlight">Some content</div>
    <p class="highlight">This is a paragraph.</p>
</body>
</html>
```

The title Attribute

It is used to provide text about an element or its content. See the following example to understand how it actually works.

```
<!DOCTYPE html>
<html lang="en">
<head>
```

```
    <meta charset="UTF-8">
    <meta HTTP-equiv="X-UA-Compatible"
content="IE=edge">
    <meta name="viewport" content="width=device-width,
initial-scale=1.0">
    <title>Document</title>
</head>
<body>
    <abbr title="World Wide Web Consortium"> W3C
</abbr>
    <a href="images-kites.jpg" title="Click to view a
larger image">
        <img src="images/kites-thumb.jpg"
alt="kites">
    </a>
</body>
</html>
```

The style Attribute

It allows to specify CSS styling rules such as color, font, border, etc. within the element. Let's check an example to see how it works.

```
<!DOCTYPE html>
<html lang="en">
<head>
    <meta charset="UTF-8">
    <meta HTTP-equiv="X-UA-Compatible"
content="IE=edge">
    <meta name="viewport" content="width=device-width,
initial-scale=1.0">
    <title>Document</title>
</head>
<body>
    <p style="color: blue;">This is a paragraph.</p>
    <img src="images/sky.jpg" style="width: 200px;"
alt="Cloudy Sky">
    <div style="border: 1px solid red;">Some content
</div>
</body>
</html>
```

MORE ABOUT STYLE ATTRIBUTES

It was designed as a simple way to present information. Its CSSs were introduced in December 1996 by the W3C to provide a good way to style elements.

CSS makes it very easy to specify things like font size and type, text and background colors, text and image alignment, the amount of space between elements, element borders and outlines, and many other styling properties.

Adding Styles to HTML Elements

It is the styling information that can either be attached as a separate document or embedded in the document itself. These are the three methods of implementing styling in an HTML document:

- Inline styles – It is used in the style attribute in the HTML start tag.

- Embedded style – It is used in the <style> element in the head section of the document.

- External style sheet – It is used in the <link> element, pointing to external CSS files.

Inline Styles

Inline styles are used to apply unique style rules to an element by inserting CSS rules directly into the start tag. It can attach to an element using the style attribute.

The style attribute contains a number of CSS property-value pairs. Each property:value pair is separated by a semicolon (;), just as you would write in an inline or external stylelist. But everything must be on one line, i.e. without a line break after a semicolon.

Example:

```
<!DOCTYPE html>
<html lang="en">
<head>
    <meta charset="UTF-8">
    <meta name="viewport" content="width=device-
width, initial-scale=1.0">
    <title>Document</title>
</head>
```

```
<body>
    <h1 style="color:red; font-size:32px;">This is
a heading</h1>
    <p style="color:green; font-size:28px;">This
is a paragraph.</p>
    <div style="color:green; font-size:18px;">This
is some text.</div>
</body>
</html>
```

Using inline styles is generally considered bad practice. Because the style rules are embedded directly in the HTML tag, it causes the presentation to blend in with the content of the document, making it very difficult to update or maintain the site.

Adding Styles to HTML Elements

Style information can be attached as a document or embedded in the document itself. There are three ways to implement style information in an HTML document:

- Inline styles – It is used to the style attribute in the HTML start tag.

- Embedded style – It is used to the <style> element in the head section of the document.

- External style sheet – It is used to the <link> element, pointing to external CSS files.

Inline Styles

Inline styles are used to apply unique style rules to an element by inserting CSS rules directly into the start tag. It can attach to an element using the style attribute. The style attribute contains a number of CSS property-value pairs. Each property:value pair is separated by a semicolon (;), just as you would write in an inline or external stylelist. But everything must be on one line, i.e. without a line break after a semicolon.

Example:

```
<!DOCTYPE HTML>
<html>
```

```
   <head>
     <meta content="text/HTML; HTTP-equiv="Content-
Type" charset=utf-8">
     <title>Title of the document</title>
     <style>
     body{
       width:500px;
       margin:0 auto,
     }
     </style>
   </head>

   <body>
     <h1> Nesting HTML Elements </h1>
     <h1 style="color:red; font-size:20px;">This is
a heading in red color with 30 font size</h1>
     <p style="color:green; font-size:28px;">This
is a paragraph in green with 18 font size </p>
     <div style="color:yellow; font-
size:28px;">This is div the text in the div will
be of yellow with 28 font </div>

   </html>
```

Embedded Style Sheets

Embedded are also called as internal style sheets that only affect the document they are embedded into. Embedded style sheets are defined in the <head> tag of the document using the <style> tag. You can define various number of <style> elements in the <head> section.

```
<!DOCTYPE HTML>
<html>
   <head>
     <meta content="text/HTML; HTTP-equiv="Content-
Type" charset=utf-8">
     <title>Title of the document</title>
     <style>
     body{
       width:500px;
       margin:0 auto;
       background-color: YellowGreen;
```

```
      }
      h1 { color: blue; }
          p { color: red; }

      </style>
   </head>

   <body>
      <h1> HTML Elements </h1>
      <h1 >This is a heading in red color with 30 font
size</h1>
      <p >This is a paragraph in green with 18 font size
</p>
      <div>This is div the text in the div will be of
yellow with 28 font </div>

   </html>
```

External Styles

An external stylesheet is used when the style is applied to many pages. An external style sheet contains all of the style rules in a separate document that you can link to from any HTML document on your website. External stylesheets are the most flexible because with an external stylesheet you can change the look of your entire site by updating just one file. You can connect external stylesheets in two ways such as linking and importing.

   Index.html

```
<!DOCTYPE HTML>
<html>
   <head>
     <meta content="text/HTML; HTTP-equiv="Content-
Type"; charset=utf-8">
     <title>Title of the document</title>
   <link href="style.css" rel="stylesheet">

   </head>

   <body>
      <h1> Nesting HTML Elements </h1>
      <h1 >This is a heading in red color with 30 font
size</h1>
```

```
    <p >This is a paragraph in green with 18 font size
</p>
    <div>This is div the text in the div will be of
yellow with 28 font </div>

</html>
```

Style.css

```
<style>
  body{
    width:500px;
    margin:0 auto;
    background-color: YellowGreen;
  }
  h1 { color: blue; }
     p { color: red; }

</style>
```

Importing External Style Sheets

The @import rule is another way to load an external stylesheet. The @import directive instructs the browser to load an external stylesheet and apply its styles.

You can use it in two ways. The easiest way is to use it in the <style> element in the <head> section. Note that additional CSS rules can still be included in the <style> element.

Example:

```
<style>
    @import URL("css/style.css");
    p {
        color: blue;
        font-size: 16px;
    }
</style>
```

Another example:

```
@import URL("css/layout.css");
@import URL("css/color.css");
```

```
body {
    color: blue;
    font-size: 14px;
}
```

HTML Image

Images improve the visual appearance of websites by making them more interesting and colorful.[16] The <img> is used to insert images into HTML documents. It is an empty element and contains only attributes. The <img> tag syntax can be specified using as below.

```
<img src="URL" alt="some_text">
```

The following is an example of images:

```
<img src="kites.jpg" alt="Flying Kites">
<img src="sky.jpg" alt="Cloudy Sky">
<img src="balloons.jpg" alt="Balloons">
```

Each image must carry at least two attributes: the src attribute and the alt attribute. The src attribute tells where to find the image. Its value is the URL of the image file. The alt attribute provides alternative text for an image if it is not available or cannot be displayed for some reason. Its value should be a meaningful replacement for the image.

More about Image Attributes

These attributes are used to specify the width and height of an image. The values of the attributes are considered in pixels by default.

```
<!DOCTYPE html>
<html lang="en">
<head>
    <meta charset="UTF-8">
    <meta HTTP-equiv="X-UA-Compatible"
content="IE=edge">
    <meta name="viewport" content="width=device-width,
initial-scale=1.0">
    <title>Document</title>
</head>
```

```
<body>
    <img src="https://images.pexels.com/
photos/12021472/pexels-photo-12021472.jpeg?auto=compre
ss&cs=tinysrgb&w=600&lazy=load" alt="Buildings"
width="300" height="300">
<img src="https://images.pexels.com/photos/13221938/
pexels-photo-13221938.jpeg?auto=compress&cs=tinysrgb&w
=600&lazy=load" alt="Mountain" width="250" height="150">
<img src="https://images.pexels.com/photos/4110404/
pexels-photo-4110404.jpeg?auto=compress&cs=tinysrgb&w=
600&lazy=load" alt="Glass" width="200" height="200">

</body>
</html>
```

You can also use the style attribute to define width and height of the images. It prevents stylesheets from changing the image size by mistake since inline style has the highest priority.

```
<!DOCTYPE html>
<html lang="en">
<head>
    <meta charset="UTF-8">
    <meta content="IE=edge"
HTTP-equiv="X-UA-Compatible">
    <meta name="viewport" content="width=device-width,
initial-scale=1.0">
    <title>Document</title>
</head>
<body>
    <img src="https://images.pexels.com/
photos/12021472/pexels-photo-12021472.jpeg?auto=compre
ss&cs=tinysrgb&w=600&lazy=load" alt="Buildings"
width="300" height="300px">
<img src="https://images.pexels.com/photos/13221938/
pexels-photo-13221938.jpeg?auto=compress&cs=tinysrgb&w
=600&lazy=load" alt="Mountain" width="250"
height="150px">
<img src="https://images.pexels.com/photos/4110404/
pexels-photo-4110404.jpeg?auto=compress&cs=tinysrgb&w=
600&lazy=load" alt="Glass" width="200" height="200px">

</body>
</html>
```

HTML TABLE

An HTML table allows you to organize data into rows and columns.[17] They are used to display tabular data such as product listings, details, financial reports, and so on.

You can create a table by using the <table> element. Inside <table>element, you can use <tr> elements to create rows, and you can use <td> elements to create columns inside a row. You can define a cell as a header for table cells using the <th> element.

The following example shows the most basic table structure:

```
<!DOCTYPE HTML>
<html>
  <head>
    <meta content="text/HTML; HTTP-equiv="Content-
Type"; charset=utf-8">
    <title>Title of the document</title>
    <style>
    body{
      width:500px;
      margin:0 auto;
      background-color: YellowGreen;
    }
    h1 { color: blue; }
        p { color: red; }

    </style>
  </head>

  <body>
   <h1> HTML Table </h1>
   <table>
    <tr>
        <th> No. </th>
        <th> Name </th>
        <th> Age </th>
    </tr>
    <tr>
        <td> 1 </td>
        <td> John </td>
        <td> 26 </td>
```

```
      </tr>
      <tr>
          <td> 2 </td>
          <td> Lim </td>
          <td> 36 </td>
      </tr>
</table>

</html>
```

By default, tables have no borders. You can use the border property to add borders to these tables. Also, table cells are sized to fit the content by default. To add space around the content in table cells, you can use the CSS padding property.

The following style rules will add a 1px border to the table and 10px padding to its cells:

```
<!DOCTYPE HTML>
<html>
   <head>
      <meta content="text/HTML; HTTP-equiv="Content-
Type"; charset=utf-8">
      <title>Title of the document</title>
      <style>
      body{
         width:500px;
         margin:0 auto;
         background-color: YellowGreen;
      }
      h1 { color: blue; }
         p { color: red; }
         table, th, td {
      border: 1px solid black;
}
th, td {
    padding: 10px;
}

      </style>
   </head>
```

```
<body>
  <h1> HTML Table </h1>
  <table>
   <tr>
       <th> No. </th>
       <th> Name </th>
       <th> Age </th>
   </tr>
   <tr>
       <td> 1 </td>
       <td> John </td>
       <td> 26 </td>
   </tr>
   <tr>
       <td> 2 </td>
       <td> Lim </td>
       <td> 36 </td>
   </tr>
</table>
</html>
```

By default, the borders around the table and its cells are separated from each other. However, you can collapse them into one using the border-collapse property of the <table> element. Text inside <th> elements is also shown in bold, aligned horizontally to the center of the cell by default. To change the default alignment, you can also use the CSS text-align property.

```
<!DOCTYPE HTML>
<html>
  <head>
    <meta content="text/HTML; HTTP-equiv="Content-
Type" charset=utf-8">
    <title>Title of the document</title>
    <style>
    body{
      width:500px;
      margin:0 auto;
      background-color: YellowGreen;
    }
```

```
    h1 { color: blue; }
        p { color: red; }
        table {
    border-collapse: collapse;
}
th {
    text-align: left;
}

    </style>
  </head>

  <body>
   <h1> HTML Table </h1>
   <table>
   <tr>
       <th> No. </th>
       <th> Name </th>
       <th> Age </th>
   </tr>
   <tr>
       <td> 1 </td>
       <td> John </td>
       <td> 26 </td>
   </tr>
   <tr>
       <td> 2 </td>
       <td> Lim </td>
       <td> 36 </td>
   </tr>
</table>

</html>
```

SPANNING MULTIPLE ROWS AND COLUMNS

Spanning allows you to extend the rows and columns of a table across multiple additional rows and columns. Normally, a table cell cannot go into the space below or above another table cell. However, you can use the rowspan or colspan attributes to span multiple rows or columns in a table.

Example:

```
<!DOCTYPE HTML>
<html>
  <head>
    <meta content="text/HTML; HTTP-equiv="Content-
Type"; charset=utf-8">
    <title>Title of the document</title>
    <style>
    body{
      width:500px;
      margin:0 auto;
      background-color: YellowGreen;
    }
    h1 { color: blue; }
        p { color: red; }
        table, th, td {
    border: 1px solid black;
}
th, td {
    padding: 10px;
}

    </style>
  </head>

  <body>
   <h1> HTML Table (col span) </h1>
   <table>
    <tr>
        <th>Name</th>
        <th colspan="2">Phone (More space done
with colspan)</th>
    </tr>
    <tr>
        <td>John Carter</td>
        <td> 5550192 </td>
        <td> 5550152 </td>
    </tr>
</table>

</html>
```

Example:

```
<!DOCTYPE HTML>
<html>
  <head>
    <meta content="text/HTML; HTTP-equiv="Content-
Type" charset=utf-8">
    <title>Title of the document</title>
    <style>
    body{
      width:500px;
      margin:0 auto;
      background-color: YellowGreen;
    }
    h1 { color: blue; }
        p { color: red; }
        table, th, td {
    border: 1px solid black;
}
th, td {
    padding: 10px;
}

    </style>
  </head>

  <body>
   <h1> HTML Table (row span) </h1>
   <table>
    <tr>
      <th rowspan="2">Phone: (more space done with
using row span)</th>
      <td>55577854</td>
   </tr>
   <tr>
       <td>55577855</td>
   </tr>
</table>

</html>
```

GIVE CAPTIONS TO TABLES

You can use the caption tag to provide a caption (or title) for your tables.

The <caption> element placed directly after the opening <table> tag. By default, it appears at the top of the table, but you can change its position using the caption-side property.

```
<!DOCTYPE HTML>
<html>
  <head>
    <meta content="text/HTML; HTTP-equiv="Content-
Type" charset=utf-8">
    <title>Title of the document</title>
    <style>
    body{
      width:500px;
      margin:0 auto;
      background-color: YellowGreen;
    }
    h1 { color: blue; }
       p { color: red; }
       table, th, td {
    border: 1px solid black;
}
th, td {
    padding: 10px;
}
    </style>
  </head>

  <body>
   <h1> HTML Table (row span) </h1>
   <table>
    <caption>Users Info</caption>
    <tr>
```

```
        <th> No </th>
        <th> Name </th>
        <th> Age </th>
    </tr>
    <tr>
        <td> 1 </td>
        <td> X </td>
        <td> Y </td>
    </tr>
    <tr>
        <td> 2 </td>
        <td> A </td>
        <td> S </td>
    </tr>
</table>

</html>
```

HTML PROPERTIES

Before diving deeper into this complete HTML book, some basics need to be clarified. As a beginner, you must be aware of the features and functions of HTML. Only then you will be able to take an interest in HTML coding. Let's discuss the important features of HTML:

- Develops the structure of the website. All the blocks and elements on the web exist because of HTML.

- Simple, human-readable tags represent elements on a web page. So they are easy to remember.

- It is universally supported by all browsers. It is a markup language for web development.

- HTML5 can provide support in improving the experience in the gaming arena.

- It is easy to learn and implement.

- It is cross-platform independent, i.e. it works on all operating systems.

WHAT TO DO WITH HTML

You can do a lot of things with HTML. It is used to publish documents online with images, lists, tables, text, etc. You can access resources such as images, videos, or other HTML documents through hyperlinks. You can create forms to collect user input such as name, email address, comments, etc. You can include sound clips, applications, and other HTML documents directly in an HTML document. You can create another offline version of your website that works without the Internet. You can store the data in the user's web browser and access it later. You can find out the current location of your website visitor.

HOW DOES HTML WORK?

Each individual HTML file contains lots of nested elements along with tags.[18] Almost anyone can write an.html file using a basic text editor and then upload it to the Internet and start creating their own web pages.

Furthermore, web data servers need to know what to do with the uploaded files and how to send them to the client's computer to understand them. HTML code is used to handle this. It's the glue that holds everything together.

Your HTML page will contain many elements that are fortunately easy to understand because they have names that describe what they are (i.e. header tags, paragraph tags, and image tags).

All websites are made up of these tags. Then your site's plain text content – what you want the user to see – is neatly wrapped in a bundle of tags that tell the page what kind of content it is. This helps the web browser understand how to display each type of content in the HTML file.

The paragraph tag puts your content into neat little paragraphs, and the header tag puts words like a proper heading on the page. You must start the tag, include the plain text content in the middle, and then close the tag so the computer knows you're done with the tag.

HTML CONTENT MODELS

In HTML5, the content of a webpage can be divided into semantic groups that describe its content. These are called content models. Each of these models describes the type of elements it contains. A content model can contain text and child elements. An element can belong to one or more content categories.

ADVANTAGES

HTML is very easy to learn and understand. HTML is the first and most important language to go through for someone learning web development. It has simple markup, and there is no case-sensitivity fuss in HTML.

It simply has some marks that serve a specific purpose and that's it. One can easily understand someone else's code and can make changes to it if necessary because there is not much to understand. Moreover, it does not cause any error or create any problem like other programming languages if the developer forgets to close the tags or makes some mistakes in the code.

One of the biggest advantages of HTML is that it is free and there is no need to buy specific software.

HTML is supported by almost every browser. HTML provides an easy way for web developers to optimize a website in HTML according to browsers.

HTML is one of the most search engine friendly compared to all the programming languages available in the market. It is much easier to create SEO-friendly websites using HTML than other programming languages. HTML web pages are easier to read and accessible to web crawlers and therefore reduce page parsing time and page load time, improving page performance.

HTML is very easy to edit because no special interface or platform is needed to edit it. It is written in simple Notepad and therefore can be easily edited in any text editor like Notepad, Notepad++, etc.

CHAPTER SUMMARY

This chapter is all about brief explanations of HTML fundamentals such as the tools and editor used to write code in HTML. Also, we write some simple code in HTML using class, id, and internal and external CSS. We will also explain the properties, features, and more.

NOTES

1. HTML – https://en.wikipedia.org/wiki/HTML#History, accessed on August 1, 2022.
2. A Brief History of HTML – https://www.washington.edu/accesscomputing/webd2/student/unit1/module3/html_history.html#:~:text=The%20first%20version%20of%20HTML,HTML%20as%20an%20XML%20language, accessed on August 1, 2022.
3. HTML History – https://en.wikipedia.org/wiki/HTML#History, accessed on August 1, 2022.

4. Why is HTML called markup language? – https://developerpitstop.com/why-is-html-called-markup-language/#:~:text=HTML%20is%20called%20a%20markup,websites%20using%20HTML%20as%20markup, accessed on August 1, 2022.

5. HTML Version list – https://www.howtocodeschool.com/2019/01/html-versions.html#HTML-2.0, accessed on August 1, 2022.

6. XHTML – https://www.geeksforgeeks.org/difference-between-xhtml-and-html5/#:~:text=XHTML%20stands%20for%20Extensible%20Hypertext,a%20better%20version%20of%20HTML, August 1, 2022.

7. HTML Basic Concepts – https://www.w3docs.com/learn-html/html-introduction.html, accessed on August 1, 2022.

8. HTML Tags – https://www.coderepublics.com/HTML/html-tags.php, accessed on August 1, 2022.

9. HTML image tag – https://www.coderepublics.com/HTML/html-tags.php, accessed on August 2, 2022.

10. HTML Tags List – https://way2tutorial.com/html/tag/index.php, accessed on August 2, 2022.

11. HTML Structure – https://www.w3docs.com/learn-html/html-introduction.html, accessed on August 2, 2022.

12. HTML Editor and Tools – https://www.hostinger.in/tutorials/best-html-editors, accessed on August 2, 2022.

13. HTML Editor and Tools – https://www.w3docs.com/learn-html/html-editors.html, accessed on August 3, 2022.

14. HTML Attributes – https://www.tutorialrepublic.com/html-tutorial/html-attributes.php, accessed on August 3, 2022.

15. HTML Common Attributes – https://www.tutorialrepublic.com/html-tutorial/html-attributes.php, accessed on August 3, 2022.

16. HTML Image – https://www.tutorialrepublic.com/html-tutorial/html-images.php, accessed on August 3, 2022.

17. HTML table – https://www.w3schools.com/html/html_tables.asp, accessed on August 3, 2022.

18. HTML Works – https://www.byjusfutureschool.com/blog/what-is-html-what-are-the-benefits-uses-features-of-html-in-real-world/, accessed on August 3, 2022.

CHAPTER 2

HTML Basic Usage

IN THIS CHAPTER

➢ The <!DOCTYPE> Declaration

➢ Common HTML elements

➢ Block-level vs. inline HTML elements

➢ Various Anatomy of HTML elements

In the previous chapter, we covered the fundamental of the HTML. Now here you will get all the basic information of HTML separately, such as all the tags and elements, along with in separate sections so that you will get to know why all these are used in HTML.

HTML TAGS

An HTML document can be described by a set of HTML tags. We'll introduce some common HTML tags that can be used to create a basic page with images, lists, tables, and links.

STRUCTURE AND TAGS OF HTML DOCUMENTS

The first thing in HTML document is the <!DOCTYPE html> tag, which specifies the correct version of HTML used throughout the document. The following shows how to use the <!DOCTYPE> tag.

ANATOMY OF AN HTML ELEMENT

Let's explore this paragraph element a little further.[1] The main parts of the element are as follows:

- **Opening tag:** It consists of the name of the element (in this case p), wrapped in opening and closing curly braces. This is where the element begins or takes effect – in this case, the paragraph begins.

- **Closing tag:** It is the same as the opening tag, which includes a slash before the element name. This is where the element ends – in this case, where the paragraph ends. Not adding a closing tag is one of the standard beginner mistakes and can lead to weird results.

- **Content:** It is the content of the element, which is just text.

- **Element:** The opening tag, closing tag, and content together form an element.

Example:

```
<!DOCTYPE HTML>
<html>
   <head>
     <meta content="text/HTML; HTTP-equiv="Content-
Type" charset=utf-8">
     <title>Title of the document</title>
     <style>
     body{
        width:500px;
        margin:0 auto;
        background-color: YellowGreen;
     }
     h1 { color: blue; }
img{
     width: 200px;
     height: 200px;
}

     </style>
   </head>
```

```
  <body>
    <h1> HTML Sample </h1>
    <!DOCTYPE html>
<html lang="en-US">
  <head>
    <meta charset="utf-8">
    <meta name="viewport"
content="width=device-width">
    <title>My test page</title>
  </head>
  <body>
    <p> This is a simple paragraph </p>
    <img src="https://images.pexels.com/
photos/11858609/pexels-photo-11858609.jpeg?auto=co
mpress&cs=tinysrgb&w=300&lazy=load" alt="My test
image">
  </body>
</html>
```

Here we have the following:

- <!DOCTYPE html> – document type. It is a mandatory preamble. Back in the mists of time when HTML was still young (around 1991/92), doctypes were supposed to act as references to a set of rules that an HTML page follows to consider good HTML, which means automatic error checking and other things. However, nowadays they do not do more and basically just need to make your document behave properly. That's all I need to know for now.

- <html> </html> – <html> element. This element wraps all content on the entire page and is sometimes called the root element. It also contains the lang attribute, which sets the primary language of the document.

- <head> </head> – <head> element. This element acts as a container for any content you want to include in your HTML page that isn't the content you're displaying to your page viewers. This includes things like keywords and page descriptions to appear in search results, Cascading Style Sheet (CSS) to style content, character set declarations, and more.

- `<meta charset="utf-8">` – It sets the character set document should use to UTF-8, which includes characters from the vast majority of written languages. Basically, it can now handle any textual content you place on it. There's no reason not to set it up, and it might help you avoid some problems later on.

- `<meta name="viewport" content="width= 'device-width'>` The viewport element ensures that the page is rendered to the width of the viewport, preventing browsers from rendering pages wider than the viewport and then scaling them down.

- `<title> </title>` – `<title>` element. It sets the title of the page, which is the name that will appear in the browser tab in which the page is loaded. It is used to describe the page when bookmark/favorite it.

- `<body> </body>` – `<body>` element. It contains all the content you want to display to web users when they visit your page, whether it's text, images, videos, games, playable audio tracks, or anything else.

Elements can have attributes that look like the ones below:

```
<p class="note"> This is an important note </p>
```

Attributes contain additional information about an element that you don't want to appear in the actual content. Class here is the name of the attribute, and editor note is the value of the attribute. The class attribute allows you to give an element a nonunique identifier that can be used to target it with style information and more.

The attribute should always have the following:

- The space between it and the element name (or the preceding attribute if the element already has one or more attributes).

- Attribute name followed by an equal sign.

- Attribute value wrapped in opening and closing quotes.

REFERENCE TO HTML ELEMENTS

The element is part of a web page.[2] In XML and HTML, an element can contain a data item or a piece of text or an image, or perhaps nothing.

A typical element includes an opening tag with some attributes, a closed body of text, and a closing tag.

They are grouped by function to help you easily find what you have in mind. An alphabetical list of all elements is available in the sidebar on each element's page and on this page.

MAIN ROOT OF HTML

<html> The <html> element represents the root (such as a top-level element) of an HTML document; therefore, it is also referred to as the main (root) element. All other elements must be children of this element.

Example:

```
<!DOCTYPE HTML>
<html>
  <head>
    <meta  content="text/HTML; HTTP-
equiv="Content-Type" charset=utf-8">
    <title>Title of the document</title>
  </head>
    <body>
    </body>
</html>
```

DOCUMENT METADATA

Metadata contains information about a page. It includes information about scripts, styles, and data that help software (search engines, browsers, etc.) use and render the page. Its styles and scripts can be defined on the page or by referencing another file that contains this information.

Example:

```
<head>
    <meta content="text/HTML; charset=utf-8" HTTP-
equiv="Content-Type" >
    <title>Title of the document</title>
  </head>
```

ELEMENT DESCRIPTION

<base> The <base> element defines the base URL to use for all relative URLs in the document. There can be one <base> element in a document.

Example:

```
<!DOCTYPE HTML>
<html>
  <head>
    <base href="https://www.pexels.com/"
target="_blank">
    <meta  content="text/HTML; HTTP-
equiv="Content-Type"  charset=utf-8">
    <title>Title of the document</title>
    <style>
        body{
            flex:1;
            width: 400px;
            margin:0 auto;
        }
    </style>
  </head>
    <body>
        <h1> Base tag</h1>
        <img src="https://images.pexels.com/
photos/8230825/pexels-photo-8230825.jpeg?auto=comp
ress&cs=tinysrgb&w=600&lazy=load" width="500"
height="500" alt="Stickman">

    </body>
</html>
```

<head> The HTML <head> element contains system-readable information (metadata) about the document, such as its title, scripts, and styles.

Example:

```
<head>
    <base href="https://www.pexels.com/"
target="_blank">
```

```
        <meta   content="text/HTML; HTTP-
    equiv="Content-Type" charset=utf-8">
        <title>Title of the document</title>
        <style>
            body{
                flex:1;
                width: 400px;
                margin:0 auto;
            }
        </style>
    </head>
```

<link> The HTML <link> element specifies relationships between the present document and an external resource. The element is most often used to interface with CSS, but it is also used to create site icons (both "favicon" style icons and icons for the home screen and apps on mobile devices) among other things.

Example:

```
<head>
    <title>of the document</title>
    </head>
```

<meta> The HTML <meta> element describes metadata that cannot be represented by other meta-related HTML elements, such as base, link, script, style, or heading.

Example:

```
<head>
    <meta   content="text/HTML; HTTP-
equiv="Content-Type"; charset=utf-8">
    </head>
```

<style> The HTML <style> element contains information about the style of a document or part of a document. It contains CSS that is applied to the content of the document containing the <style> element.

Example:

```
<head>
    <style>
        body{
            flex:1;
            width: 400px;
            margin:0 auto;
        }
    </style>
</head>
```

<title> The HTML <title> element displays the title of the document that is displayed in the browser header or page tab. It contains text only; tags in the element are ignored.

```
<head>
    <title>Title of the document</title>
</head>
```

WAY TO SEPARATE THE ROOT IN HTML

<body> The <body> HTML element displays the content of an HTML document. There can be just one <body> element in a document.

```
<body>
        <h1> Body tag</h1>
        <img src="https://images.pexels.com/
photos/8230825/pexels-photo-8230825.jpeg?auto=compress
&cs=tinysrgb&w=600&lazy=load" width="500" height="500"
alt="Stickman">

    </body>
```

CONTENT SECTIONING IN HTML

Content division elements allow you to organize the content of a document into logical parts. Use section elements to create a broad outline of page content, including header and footer navigation and title elements to identify content sections.

<address> The HTML <address> element indicates that the attached HTML code provides contact information for a person, the people, or an organization.

```
<!DOCTYPE HTML>
<html>
  <head>
    <base href="https://www.pexels.com/"
target="_blank">
    <meta  content="text/HTML; HTTP-equiv="Content-
Type" charset=utf-8">
    <title>Title of the document</title>
    <style>
        body{
            flex:1;
            width: 400px;
            margin:0 auto;
        }
    </style>
  </head>
    <body>
        <h1> Address tag</h1>
        <address>
            Written by <a href="mailto:webmaster@
example.com"> XYZ </a>.<br>
            Visit us at XYZ Place:<br>
            Contact: xyz@gmail.com<br>
            Address: Box 564, Disneyland<br>
            USA
            </address>
    </body>
</html>
```

<article> The HTML <article> element represents a separate composition in a document, page, application, or website that is intended to be distributed or reused (e.g., in syndication). Examples: a magazine or newspaper article or blog post, a product details, a user-submitted comment, a widget or gadget, or other independent content.

```
<!DOCTYPE HTML>
<html>
```

```
<head>
  <base href="https://www.pexels.com/"
target="_blank">
  <meta  content="text/HTML; HTTP-equiv="Content-
Type" charset=utf-8">
  <title>Title of the document</title>
  <style>
      body{
          flex:1;
          width: 400px;
          margin:0 auto;
      }
  </style>
</head>
  <body>
      <h1> Article tag</h1>
      <article>
          <h2> HTML </h2>
          <p> HTML stands for HyperText Markup
Language. It is a markup language for web page
creation. </p>
      </article>

      <article>
          <h2> CSS </h2>
          <p> CSS stands for Cascading Style Sheets.
It describes how elements are to be displayed on
screen, paper, or in other media. </p>
      </article>

      <article>
          <h2> JavaScript </h2>
          <p>Javascript is used across the world to
create dynamic and interactive web content like
applications and browsers</p>
      </article>
  </body>
</html>
```

<aside> The HTML <aside> element represents a part of a document whose content is only indirectly related to the content of the document. Asides are often presented as sidebars or callouts.

Example:

```
<!DOCTYPE HTML>
<html>
  <head>
    <base href="https://www.pexels.com/"
target="_blank">
    <meta  content="text/HTML; HTTP-
equiv="Content-Type";  charset=utf-8">
    <title>Title of the document</title>
    <style>
        body{
            flex:1;
            width: 400px;
            margin:0 auto;
        }
    </style>
  </head>
    <body>
        <h1> Aside tag</h1>
        <aside>
            <h4> XYZ Text </h4>
            <p> Curabitur lacinia lectus ut quam
tincidunt, sit amet commodo dolor pharetra. </p>
          </aside>
          <aside>
            <h4>XYZ Text </h4>
            <p> Curabitur lacinia lectus ut quam
tincidunt, sit amet commodo dolor pharetra.
            </p>
          </aside>
      </body>
</html>
```

<footer> The HTML <footer> element represents the footer for its closest content-splitting ancestor or the root division element. The <footer> contains information about the author of the section, copyright information, or links to related documents.

Example:

```
<!DOCTYPE HTML>
<html>
  <head>
    <base href="https://www.pexels.com/"
target="_blank">
    <meta content="text/HTML;    HTTP-
equiv="Content-Type" charset=utf-8">
    <title>Title of the document</title>
    <style>
        body{
            flex:1;
            width: 600px;
            margin:0 auto;
        }
        footer{
            border:1px solid black;
            padding:10px;
            background: pink;
        }
    </style>
  </head>
    <body>
        <h1> Aside tag</h1>
        <aside>
            <h4> XYZ Text </h4>
            <p> Curabitur lacinia lectus ut quam
tincidunt, sit amet commodo dolor pharetra. </p>
        </aside>
        <aside>
            <h4>XYZ Text </h4>
            <p> Curabitur lacinia lectus ut quam
tincidunt, sit amet commodo dolor pharetra.
            </p>
        </aside>
        <footer>
            <h2> Footer tag </h2>
            <p>Author: Hege Refsnes<br>
            <a href="mailto:hege@example.com">
hege@example.com</a></p>
        </footer>
    </body>
</html>
```

<header> The HTML <header> element represents introductory content, usually a group of introductory or navigation aids. It can contain some elements of the title, but also a logo, a search form, the name of the author, and other elements.

Example:

```
<!DOCTYPE HTML>
<html>
  <head>
    <base href="https://www.pexels.com/"
target="_blank">
    <meta   content="text/HTML;
HTTP-equiv="Content-Type"charset=utf-8">
    <title>Title of the document</title>
    <style>
        body{
            flex:1;
            width: 600px;
            margin:0 auto;
        }
        footer{
            border:1px solid black;
            padding:10px;
            background: pink;
        }
        header{
            border:1px solid black;
            padding:10px;
            background: blue;
        }
    </style>
  </head>
    <body>
            <header>
              <h1>A heading here</h1>
              <p>Posted by John Doe</p>
              <p>Some additional information
here</p>
            </header>
            <p>Lorem Ipsum dolor set amet....</p>
```

```
            <aside>
                <h4> XYZ Text </h4>
                <p> Curabitur lacinia lectus ut quam
tincidunt, sit amet commodo dolor pharetra. </p>
            </aside>
            <aside>
                <h4>XYZ Text </h4>
                <p> Curabitur lacinia lectus ut quam
tincidunt, sit amet commodo dolor pharetra.
                </p>
            </aside>
            <footer>
                <h2> Footer tag </h2>
                <p>Author: Hege Refsnes<br>
                <a href="mailto:hege@example.com">
hege@example.com</a></p>
            </footer>
        </body>
</html>
```

<h1>, <h2>, <h3>, <h4>, <h5>, <h6> HTML elements <h1> through <h6> represent six levels of section headings. <h1> is the top level of the section and <h6> is the lowest.

Example:

```
<!DOCTYPE HTML>
<html>
   <head>
     <base href="https://www.pexels.com/"
target="_blank">
     <meta content="text/HTML; HTTP-equiv="Content-
Type" charset=utf-8">
     <title>Title of the document</title>
     <style>
        body{
            flex:1;
            width: 600px;
            margin:0 auto;
        }
        p{
```

```
            font-size: 34px;
        }
    </style>
  </head>
    <body>
        <p> Heading Tags </p>
            <h1> Heading 1 </h1>
            <h2>  Heading 2 </h2>
            <h3>  Heading 3 </h3>
            <h5>  Heading 4 </h5>
            <h6>  Heading 5 </h6>
    </body>
  </html>
```

<main> The HTML <main> element represents the content of the body of the document. The content consists of content that directly relates to or extends the central topic of the document or the central function of the application.

```
<!DOCTYPE HTML>
<html>
  <head>
    <base href="https://www.pexels.com/"
target="_blank">
    <meta  content="text/HTML; HTTP-equiv="Content-
Type" charset=utf-8">
    <title>Title of the document</title>
    <style>
        body{
            flex:1;
            width: 700px;
            margin:0 auto;
        }
        footer{
            border:1px solid black;
            padding:10px;
            background: pink;
        }
        header{
            border:1px solid black;
            padding:10px;
```

```
        background: blue;
    }
    main{
        padding:10px;
        background-color:lightcoral;
        height:350px
    }
  </style>
 </head>
  <body>
        <header>
          <h1> Header tag </h1>
          <p>Posted by John Doe</p>
          <p>Some additional information here</p>
        </header>
        <main>
            <h1>Here is the main content of the
page</h1>
            <aside>
                <h4> XYZ Text </h4>
                <p> Curabitur lacinia lectus ut
quam tincidunt, sit amet commodo dolor pharetra. </p>
            </aside>
            <aside>
                <h4>XYZ Text </h4>
                <p> Curabitur lacinia lectus ut
quam tincidunt, sit amet commodo dolor pharetra.
                </p>
            </aside>
        </main>

        <footer>
          <h1> Footer tag </h1>
          <p>Author: Hege Refsnes<br>
          <a href="mailto:hege@example.com">
hege@example.com</a></p>
        </footer>
    </body>
  </html>
```

<nav> The HTML <nav> element represents a part of a page whose pur-
pose is to provide navigational links, either within the current document

or to other documents. Common examples of navigation sections are menus, table of contents, and indexes.

```
<!DOCTYPE html>
<html>
<head>
<style>
nav {
  list-style-type: none;
  margin: 0;
  padding: 0px;
  overflow: hidden;
  background-color: lightgray;
}

li {
  float: left;
    border-right: 1px solid blue;
}

li a {
  display: block;
  color: blue;
 font-size:20px;
  text-align: center;
  padding: 10px 20px;
  text-decoration: none;
}
.active{
background-color: gray;
color: white;
}
li a:hover {
  background-color: orange;
  color: white;
}
footer{
        border:1px solid black;
        padding:10px;
        background: pink;
    }
```

```
        header{
            border:1px solid black;
            padding:10px;
            background: WhiteSmoke;
        }
        main{
            padding:10px;
            background-color:lightcoral;
            height:400px
        }

</style>
</head>
<body>


<header>
    <h2> Nav Tag </h2>
    <nav>
        <li><a class="active" href="#home">Home</a>
</li>
        <li><a href="#">Java</a></li>
        <li><a href="#">HTML</a></li>
        <li><a href="#">CSS</a></li>
      </nav>
   </header>
   <main>
       <h1>Here is the main content of the page</h1>
       <aside>
           <h4> XYZ Text </h4>
           <p> Curabitur lacinia lectus ut quam
tincidunt, sit amet commodo dolor pharetra. </p>
       </aside>
       <aside>
           <h4>XYZ Text </h4>
           <p> Curabitur lacinia lectus ut quam
tincidunt, sit amet commodo dolor pharetra.
        </p>
        </aside>
   </main>
```

```
<footer>
  <h1> Footer tag </h1>
  <p>Author: Hege Refsnes<br>
  <a href="mailto:hege@example.com">hege@example.com
</a></p>
</footer>

</body>
</html>
```

<section> The HTML <section> element shows a generic stand-alone section of a document that does not have a more specific element to represent it. The sections should always have a heading, with very few exceptions.

Example:

```
<!DOCTYPE html>
<html>
<head>
<style>
nav {
   list-style-type: none;
   margin: 0;
   padding: 0px;
   overflow: hidden;
   background-color: lightgray;
}

li {
   float: left;
      border-right: 1px solid blue;
}

li a {
   display: block;
   color: blue;
 font-size:20px;
   text-align: center;
   padding: 10px 20px;
   text-decoration: none;
}
```

```
.active{
background-color: gray;
color: white;
}
li a:hover {
  background-color: orange;
  color: white;
}
footer{
          border:1px solid black;
          padding:10px;
          background: pink;
      }
      header{
          border:1px solid black;
          padding:10px;
          background: WhiteSmoke;
      }
      main{
          padding:10px;
          background-color:lightcoral;
          height:400px
      }

</style>
</head>
<body>


<header>
    <h2> Header Tag </h2>
  </header>
  <main>
      <h3> Section tag under main tag</h3>
      <section>
          <h4> XYZ Text </h4>
          <p> Curabitur lacinia lectus ut quam
tincidunt, sit amet commodo dolor pharetra. </p>
      </section>
      <section>
          <h4>XYZ Text </h4>
```

```
          <p> Curabitur lacinia lectus ut quam
tincidunt, sit amet commodo dolor pharetra.
          </p>
        </section>
    </main>

<footer>
  <h1> Footer tag </h1>
</footer>

</body>
</html>
```

TEXTUAL CONTENT

Use textual content elements to organize blocks or pieces of content placed between the opening <body> tag and the closing </body> tag. These elements are important for accessibility and Search Engine Optimization (SEO) because they identify the purpose or structure of the content.

<blockquote> The HTML <blockquote> element indicates that the enclosed text is an extended quotation. This is usually rendered visually by indentation. The URL for the source of the citation can be specified using the cite attribute, while the textual representation of the source can be specified using the cite element.

Example:

```
<!DOCTYPE html>
<html>
<head>
<style>
main{
  padding:10px;
  background-color:lightcoral;
  height:400px
}

</style>
</head>
<body>
  <main>
```

```
        <h3> Section tag under main tag</h3>
        <blockquote cite="http://www.worldwildlife.
org/who/index.html">
        Curabitur lacinia lectus ut quam
tincidunt, sit amet commodo dolor pharetra.
        </blockquote>
     </main>
  </body>
  </html>
```

<dd> The HTML <dd> element provides a description, definition, or value for the preceding expression (dt) in a list of descriptions (dl).

```
<!DOCTYPE html>
<html>
<head>
<style>
main{
  padding:10px;
  background-color:lightcoral;
  height:400px
}

</style>
</head>
<body>
  <main>
    <dl>
      <dt> 1 HTML </dt>
      <dd> Hyper Text Makrup Language </dd>
      <dt> CSS </dt>
      <dd> Cascading Style Sheet </dd>
    </dl>
    </main>
</body>
</html>
```

<div> The HTML <div> element is a general container for the content of a stream. It has no effect on content or layout until it's modified in some way with CSS (e.g., styled directly on it or some kind of layout model like Flexbox applied to its parent). It is used inside paragraphs, line breaks, images, links, lists, etc.

Example:

```
<!DOCTYPE html>
<html>
<head>
<style>
div{
   padding:10px;
   background-color:lightcoral;
   width:400px;
   background-color: lightcoral;
   margin:0 auto;
   border: 1px solid black;
}

</style>
</head>
<body>
   <main>
      <div>
         <h3> Div tag</h3>
         Curabitur lacinia lectus ut quam tincidunt,
sit amet commodo dolor pharetra.
      </div>

      <div>
         <h3> Div tag</h3>
         Curabitur lacinia lectus ut quam
tincidunt, sit amet commodo dolor pharetra.
      </div>
   </main>
</body>
</html>
```

<dl> The HTML <dl> element represents a list of descriptions. The element contains a list of groups of terms (specified by the dt element) and descriptions (provided by the dd element). A common use of this element is to implement a glossary or to display metadata (a list of key-value pairs).

```
!DOCTYPE html>
<html>
<head>
```

```
<style>
main{
  padding:10px;
  background-color:lightcoral;
  height:400px
}

</style>
</head>
<body>
  <main>
    <dl>
      <dt> 1 HTML </dt>
      <dd> Hyper Text Makrup Language </dd>
      <dt> CSS </dt>
      <dd> Cascading Style Sheet </dd>
    </dl>
    </main>
</body>
</html>
```

<dt> The HTML <dt> element specifies a term in a list of descriptions or definitions and as such must be used inside the dl element. It is usually followed by a dd element; multiple <dt> elements in a row indicate multiple expressions that are all defined by the immediately following dd element.

```
!DOCTYPE html>
<html>
<head>
<style>
main{
  padding:10px;
  background-color:lightcoral;
  height:400px
}

</style>
</head>
<body>
  <main>
```

```
      <dl>
        <dt> 1 HTML </dt>
        <dd> Hyper Text Makrup Language </dd>
        <dt> CSS </dt>
        <dd> Cascading Style Sheet </dd>
      </dl>
      </main>
</body>
</html>
```

<figcaption> The HTML <figcaption> element represents a caption or legend describing the rest of the content of its parent image element.

```
<!DOCTYPE html>
<html>
<head>
<style>
div{
  padding:10px;
  width:400px;
  margin:0 auto;
  width: 500px;
  height:400px
}
h1{
  text-align: center;
}

</style>
</head>
<body>
  <div>
    <h1> Figure Tag </h1>
    <figure>
      <img src="https://images.pexels.com/
photos/638479/pexels-photo-638479.jpeg?auto=compress&
cs=tinysrgb&w=600" alt="Trulli" style="width:100%">
      <figcaption>Fig.1 - Car </figcaption>
    </figure>
  </div>
</body>
</html>
```

<figure> The HTML <figure> element represents a separate content, possibly with an optional caption, which is specified using the figcaption element. The image, its caption, and its content are linked as a single entity.

```
<!DOCTYPE html>
<html>
<head>
<style>
div{
  padding:10px;
  width:400px;
  margin:0 auto;
  width: 500px;
  height:400px
}
h1{
  text-align: center;
}

</style>
</head>
<body>
  <div>
    <h1> Figure Tag </h1>
    <figure>
      <img src="https://images.pexels.com/
photos/638479/pexels-photo-638479.jpeg?auto=compress&
cs=tinysrgb&w=600" alt="Trulli" style="width:100%">
      <figcaption>Fig.1 - Car </figcaption>
    </figure>
  </div>
</body>
</html>
```

<hr> The HTML <hr> element represents a thematic break in-between paragraph-level elements; for example, a scene change in a film or a topic shift within a section.

Example:

```
<!DOCTYPE html>
<html>
```

```
<head>
<style>
body{
  padding:10px;
  width:400px;
  margin:0 auto;
}
h1{
  text-align: center;
}
hr{
  width:80%
}
</style>
</head>
<body>
  <h1> hr tag </h1>
    <p>
      Curabitur lacinia lectus ut quam tincidunt,
sit amet commodo dolor pharetra.
    </p>
<hr>
    <p>
      Curabitur lacinia lectus ut quam tincidunt,
sit amet commodo dolor pharetra.
    </p>
</body>
</html>
```

<li> The HTML <li> element is used to represent an item in a list. It can be contained in a parent element such as an ordered list (ol), an unordered list (ul), or a menu (menu). In unordered lists, list items are displayed using bullets. In ordered lists, they usually appear with an ascending counter to the left, such as a number or letter.

Example:

```
<!DOCTYPE html>
<html>
<head>
<style>
```

```
body{
  padding:10px;
  width:400px;
  margin:0 auto;
}
h1{
  text-align: center;
}
hr{
  width:80%
}
</style>
</head>
<body>
  <h1> ol and ul tag </h1>
  <p>The ol element defines an ordered list:</p>
  <ol>
    <li> HTML </li>
    <li> CSS </li>
    <li> JavaScript </li>
  </ol>

  <p>The ul element defines an unordered list:</p>
  <ul>
    <li> HTML </li>
    <li> CSS </li>
    <li> JavaScript </li>
  </ul>
</body>
</html>
```

<menu> The HTML <menu> element is described in the specification as a semantic alternative to ul, but browsers do not differentiate it (and exposed it via the accessibility tree) from ul. It represents an unordered list of items (which is represented by li elements).

<ol> The <ol> element represents an ordered list of items – usually rendered as a numbered list.

```
<!DOCTYPE html>
<html>
<head>
```

```
<style>
body{
  padding:10px;
  width:400px;
  margin:0 auto;
}
h1{
  text-align: center;
}
hr{
  width:80%
}
</style>
</head>
<body>
  <h1> ol and ul tag </h1>
  <p>The ol element defines an ordered list:</p>
  <ol>
    <li> HTML </li>
    <li> CSS </li>
    <li> JavaScript </li>
  </ol>
</body>
</html>
```

<p> The HTML <p> element represents a paragraph. Paragraphs are typically represented in visual media as blocks of text separated from adjacent blocks by blank lines and/or first-line indentation, but paragraphs can be any structural grouping of related content, such as images or form fields.

Example:

```
<!DOCTYPE html>
<html>
<head>
<style>
body{
  padding:10px;
  width:400px;
  margin:0 auto;
}
```

```
h1{
   text-align: center;
}

</style>
</head>
<body>
  <h1> p tag </h1>
    <p>
       Curabitur lacinia lectus ut quam tincidunt,
sit amet commodo dolor pharetra.
    </p>
    <p>
       Curabitur lacinia lectus ut quam tincidunt,
sit amet commodo dolor pharetra.
    </p>
</body>
</html>
```

<pre> The HTML <pre> element represents preformatted text to be presented exactly as written in the HTML file. Text is usually rendered using a proportional or nonproportional font. A space inside this element will appear as typed.

Example:

```
<!DOCTYPE html>
<html>
<head>
<style>
body{
   padding:10px;
   width:400px;
   margin:0 auto;
}
h1{
   text-align: center;
}

</style>
</head>
```

```
<body>
  <h1> pre tag </h1>
    <pre>
      Curabitur lacinia lectus ut quam tincidunt,
sit amet commodo dolor pharetra.
      Curabitur lacinia lectus ut quam tincidunt,
sit amet commodo dolor pharetra.
    </pre>
</body>
</html>
```

<ul> The HTML <ul> element defines an unordered list of items, usually rendered as a bulleted list.

Example:

```
<!DOCTYPE html>
<html>
<head>
<style>
body{
  padding:10px;
  width:400px;
  margin:0 auto;
}
h1{
  text-align: center;
}
hr{
  width:80%
}
</style>
</head>
<body>
  <h1> ol and ul tag </h1>
  <p>The ol element defines an ordered list:</p>
  <ol>
    <li> HTML </li>
    <li> CSS </li>
    <li> JavaScript </li>
  </ol>
```

```
<p>The ul element defines an unordered list:</p>
<ul>
  <li> HTML </li>
  <li> CSS </li>
  <li> JavaScript </li>
</ul>
</body>
</html>
```

SEMANTICS OF EMBEDDED TEXT

Use HTML inline text semantics to define the meaning, structure, or style of a word, line, or any text.

<a> The HTML <a> element (or anchor element) with href attribute creates a hyperlink to pages, files, emails, locations on the particular page, or anything else that a URL can address.

Example:

```
<!DOCTYPE html>
<html>
<head>
<style>
nav {
  list-style-type: none;
  margin: 0;
  padding: 0px;
  overflow: hidden;
  background-color: lightgray;
}

li {
  float: left;
    border-right: 1px solid blue;
}

li a {
  display: block;
  color: blue;
 font-size:20px;
  text-align: center;
  padding: 10px 20px;
```

```
  text-decoration: none;
}
.active{
background-color: gray;
color: white;
}
li a:hover {
  background-color: orange;
  color: white;
}

</style>
</head>
<body>


<header>
    <h2> Nav Tag </h2>
    <nav>
        <li><a class="active" href="#home">Home
</a></li>
        <li><a href="#">Java</a></li>
        <li><a href="#">HTML</a></li>
        <li><a href="#">CSS</a></li>
      </nav>
   </header>

</body>
</html>
```

<abbr> The HTML <abbr> element defines an abbreviation or acronym.

Example:

```
<!DOCTYPE html>
<html>
<head>
<style>
nav {
  list-style-type: none;
```

```
      margin: 0;
      padding: 0px;
      overflow: hidden;
      background-color: lightgray;
}

li {
   float: left;
      border-right: 1px solid blue;
}

li a {
   display: block;
   color: blue;
  font-size:20px;
   text-align: center;
   padding: 10px 20px;
   text-decoration: none;
}
.active{
background-color: gray;
color: white;
}
li a:hover {
   background-color: orange;
   color: white;
}

</style>
</head>
<body>

   <p>You can use <abbr>CSS</abbr> (Cascading Style
Sheets) to style your <abbr>HTML</abbr> (HyperText
Markup Language). Using style sheets, you can keep
your <abbr>CSS</abbr> presentation layer and
<abbr>HTML</abbr> content layer separate. This is
called "separation of concerns."</p>

</body>
</html>
```

<b> The HTML <b> element is used to draw the reader's attention to the content of an element that is otherwise given no particular meaning. This was formerly known as the Boldface element, and the most browsers draw text in bold. However, you cannot use <b> to style text; instead, you should use the CSS font-weight property to make the text bold, or the strong element to indicate that the text has special importance.

Example:

```
<!DOCTYPE html>
<html>
<head>
<style>
div {
   list-style-type: none;
   margin: 0;
   padding: 0px;
   overflow: hidden;
}

li {
   float: left;
     border-right: 1px solid black;
     color:black;
}

li a {
   display: block;
 font-size:20px;
   text-align: center;
   padding: 10px 20px;
   text-decoration: none;
   color:black;

}

</style>
</head>
<body>
```

```
<header>
    <h2> Normal text   </h2>
    <div>
        <li><a class="active" href="#home">Home</
a></li>
        <li><a href="#">Java</a></li>
        <li><a href="#">HTML</a></li>
        <li><a href="#">CSS</a></li>
    </div>

    <h2> Bold tag </h2>
    <div>
        <li><a class="active" href="#home"> <b>
Home </b></a></li>
        <li><a href="#">   <b> Java </b></a></li>
        <li><a href="#">   <b> HTML </b> </a></li>
        <li><a href="#">   <b> CSS </b> </a></li>
    </div>
  </header>

</body>
</html>
```

<bdi> The HTML <bdi> element tells the browser's two-way algorithm to treat the text it contains in isolation from the surrounding text. This is especially useful when the website dynamically inserts some text and does not know the directionality of the inserted text.

Bidirectional text is the text that may contain both sequences of characters that are arranged left-to-right (LTR) and sequences of characters that are arranged right-to-left (RTL), such as an Arabic quotation embedded in an English string.

Example:

```
<!DOCTYPE html>
<html>
<head>
<style>
div {
  list-style-type: none;
  margin: 0;
```

```
   padding: 0px;
   overflow: hidden;
}

HTML {
    font-family: sans-serif;
}

bdi {

}

.name {
    color: red;
}

</style>
</head>
<body>


   <h1> bdi tag </h1>

   <ul>
      <li><bdi class="name">Evil Steven</bdi>: 1st
place</li>
      <li><bdi class="name">François fatale</bdi>:
2nd place</li>
      <li><span class="name">تیز سمی</span>: 3rd
place</li>
      <li><bdi class="name">الرجل القوي إیان</bdi>: 4th
place</li>
      <li><span class="name" dir="auto">تیز سمی
</span>: 5th place</li>
   </ul>

</body>
</html>
```

<bdo> The HTML <bdo> element overrides the current text orientation so that the text inside is rendered in a different direction.

 The HTML <br> element creates a line break in the text (carriage-return). It is useful when writing a poem or an address, where there are significant line breaks.

Example:

```
<!DOCTYPE html>
<html>
<head>
<style>
body{
  padding:10px;
  width:400px;
  margin:0 auto;
}
h1{
  text-align: center;
}

</style>
</head>
<body>
  <h1> p tag </h1>
    <p>
       Curabitur lacinia lectus ut quam tincidunt,
sit amet commodo dolor pharetra.
    </p>
    <br />
    <p>
       Curabitur lacinia lectus ut quam tincidunt,
sit amet commodo dolor pharetra.
    </p>
</body>
</html>
```

<cite> The HTML <cite> element is used to describe a link to a cited creative work and must contain the title of that work. The link may be abbreviated in accordance with context-appropriate citation metadata conventions.

Example:

```
<!DOCTYPE html>
<html>
```

```
<head>
<style>
body{
  padding:10px;
  width:400px;
  margin:0 auto;
}
h1{
  text-align: center;
}

</style>
</head>
<body>
  <h1> cite tag </h1>
  <figure>
    <blockquote>
        <p>Lorem ipsum dolor sit amet, consectetur
adipiscing elit.</p>
    </blockquote>
    <figcaption> We pick first sentence from
<cite><a href="http://www.george-orwell.
org/1984/0.html"> Lorem Site </a></cite>
</figcaption>
  </figure>
</body>
</html>
```

<code> The HTML <code> element displays its content styled in a way that is intended to indicate the text is a short fragment of code. By default, the content text is displayed using the user agent's default monospaced font.

Example:

```
<!DOCTYPE html>
<html>
<head>
<style>
body{
  padding:10px;
```

```
    width:400px;
    margin:0 auto;
}
h1{
    text-align: center;
}

</style>
</head>
<body>
    <h1> code tag </h1>
    <p>The <code>push()</code> method adds more than
elements to the end of an array and returns the
new length of the array.</p>
</body>
</html>
```

<data> The HTML <data> element links a given piece of content to a machine-readable translation. If the content is time or date related, the time element must be used.

Example:

```
<!DOCTYPE html>
<html>
<head>
<style>
body{
    padding:10px;
    width:400px;
    margin:0 auto;
}
h1{
    text-align: center;
}

</style>
</head>
<body>
    <h1> data tag </h1>
    <p>  Programming Language </p>
```

```
<ul>
    <li><data value="1"> HTML </data></li>
    <li><data value="2"> CSS </data></li>
    <li><data value="3"> PHP </data></li>
</ul>
</body>
</html>
```

<dfn> The HTML <dfn> element is used to mark a term that is defined in the context of a defining phrase or sentence. A p element, a dt/dd pairing, or a section element that is the closest ancestor of <dfn> is treated as a term definition.

Example:

```
<!DOCTYPE html>
<html>
<head>
<style>
body{
   padding:10px;
   width:400px;
   margin:0 auto;
}
h1{
   text-align: center;
}

</style>
</head>
<body>
   <h1> dfn tag </h1>
   <p>A <dfn id="def-validator">validator</dfn> is
a program that checks for syntax errors in code or
documents.</p>
   </body>
</html>
```

<em> The HTML <em> element indicates text that is highlighted. The <em> element can nest, with each level of nesting indicating a greater degree of emphasis.

Example:

```
<!DOCTYPE html>
<html>
<head>
<style>
body{
  padding:10px;
  width:400px;
  margin:0 auto;
}
h1{
  text-align: center;
}
em{
  border-bottom: 1px solid green;
}

</style>
</head>
<body>
  <h1> p tag </h1>
    <p>
      Curabitur lacinia lectus ut quam tincidunt,
<em>Lorem</em> sit amet commodo dolor pharetra.
Curabitur lacinia lectus ut quam tincidunt, sit
amet commodo dolor pharetra.
    </p>

</body>
</html>
```

<i> The HTML <i> element represents a range of text that differs from normal text for some reason, such as text, technical terms, taxonomic labels, among others. Historically, this data was shown in italics, which is the original source of the <i> naming of this element.

Example:

```
<!DOCTYPE html>
<html>
<head>
```

```
<style>
body{
  padding:10px;
  width:400px;
  margin:0 auto;
}
h1{
  text-align: center;
}
em{
  border-bottom: 1px solid green;
}

</style>
</head>
<body>
  <h1> i tag </h1>
    <i>
      Curabitur lacinia lectus ut quam tincidunt,
Lorem sit amet commodo dolor pharetra.Curabitur
lacinia lectus ut quam tincidunt, sit amet commodo
dolor pharetra.
</i>

</body>
</html>
```

<kbd> The HTML <kbd> element represents a range of embedded text indicating textual user input from a keyboard, voice note, or any other text input device. By convention, the user agent renders the content of the <kbd> element using its default monospaced font by default, although the HTML standard does not mandate this.

Example:

```
<!DOCTYPE html>
<html>
<head>
<style>
body{
  padding:10px;
```

```
    width:400px;
    margin:0 auto;
}
h1{
    text-align: center;
}
em{
    border-bottom: 1px solid green;
}

</style>
</head>
<body>
    <h1> kbd tag </h1>
    <p> Please press <kbd>Ctrl</kbd> + <kbd> C
</kbd>  to  copy any content. </p>
    <p> Please press <kbd>Ctrl</kbd> + <kbd> X
</kbd>  to  cut any content. </p>
    <p> Please press <kbd>Ctrl</kbd> + <kbd> V
</kbd>  to  paste any content. </p>
</body>
</html>
```

<mark> The HTML <mark> element represents text that is marked or highlighted for reference or notation purposes because of the relevance or importance of the marked passage in the accompanying context.

Example:

```
<!DOCTYPE html>
<html>
<head>
<style>
body{
    padding:10px;
    width:400px;
    margin:0 auto;
}
h1{
    text-align: center;
}
```

```
em{
   border-bottom: 1px solid green;
}

</style>
</head>
<body>
   <h1> mark tag </h1>
<p> <mark> Lorem </mark> ipsum dolor sit amet,
consectetur adipiscing elit. Cras id tincidunt
dui. Fusce congue metus leo, vitae condimentum
purus malesuada vel.</p>
<p><mark> Lorem </mark> ipsum dolor sit amet,
consectetur adipiscing elit. Cras id tincidunt
dui. Fusce congue metus leo, vitae condimentum
purus malesuada vel.</p>
</body>
</html>
```

<q> The HTML <q> element indicates that the attached text is a short-embedded citation. Most modern browsers are implemented by surrounding the text with quotation marks. This element is intended for short citations that do not require paragraph breaks; use the blockquote element for long quotes.

```
<!DOCTYPE html>
<html>
<head>
<style>
body{
   padding:10px;
   width:400px;
   margin:0 auto;
}
h1{
   text-align: center;
}
em{
   border-bottom: 1px solid green;
}

</style>
</head>
```

```
<body>
  <h1> q tag </h1>
  <p>Inspirational Quotes : <q>Keep smiling, because
life is a beautiful thing and there's so much to smile
about. </q></p>
</body>
</html>
```

<rp> The HTML <rp> element is used to provide fallback brackets for browsers that do not support displaying ruby annotations using the ruby element. A single <rp> element should enclose each of the opening and closing brackets that wrap the <rp> element that contains the annotation text.

Example:

```
<!DOCTYPE html>
<html>
<head>
<style>
body{
  padding:10px;
  width:400px;
  margin:0 auto;
}
h1{
  text-align: center;
}
em{
  border-bottom: 1px solid green;
}

</style>
</head>
<body>
  <h1> rp tag </h1>
  <ruby>
   <p> 漢 <rp>(</rp><rt>ㄏㄢˋ</rt><rp>)</rp> </p>
   <p> 漢 <rp>(</rp><rt>kan</rt><rp>)</rp> </p>
   <p> 字 <rp>(</rp><rt>ji</rt><rp>)</rp> </p>
   </ruby>
  </body>
</html>
```

<rt> The HTML <rt> element specifies a ruby annotation ruby text component that is used to provide pronunciation, translation, or transliteration information for Asian typography. The <rt> element always be contained within a ruby element.

```
<!DOCTYPE html>

<html>
<head>
<style>
body{
  padding:10px;
  width:400px;
  margin:0 auto;
}
h1{
  text-align: center;
}
em{
  border-bottom: 1px solid green;
}

</style>
</head>
<body>
  <h1> rp tag </h1>
  <ruby>
    <p> 漢 <rp>(</rp><rt>ㄏㄢˋ</rt><rp>)</rp> </p>
     <p> 漢 <rp>(</rp><rt>kan</rt><rp>)</rp> </p>
     <p> 字 <rp>(</rp><rt>ji</rt><rp>)</rp> </p>
     </ruby>
   </body>
</html>
```

<ruby> The HTML <ruby> element represents annotations that rendered above, below, or next to the body text, typically used to display the pronunciation of East Asian characters. It can also be used to annotate other kinds of text, but this use is less common.

```
<!DOCTYPE html>
<html>
```

```
<head>
<style>
body{
  padding:10px;
  width:400px;
  margin:0 auto;
}
h1{
  text-align: center;
}
em{
  border-bottom: 1px solid green;
}

</style>
</head>
<body>
  <h1> rp tag </h1>
  <ruby>
   <p> 漢 <rp>(</rp><rt>ㄏㄢˋ</rt><rp>)</rp> </p>
    <p> 漢 <rp>(</rp><rt>kan</rt><rp>)</rp> </p>
    <p> 字 <rp>(</rp><rt>ji</rt><rp>)</rp> </p>
    </ruby>
  </body>
</html>
```

<s> The HTML <s> element renders text with a strike through or strikethrough line. Use the <s> element to display things that are no longer relevant or accurate. However, <s> is not appropriate when marking document edits; use del and ins elements for this as needed.

Example:

```
<!DOCTYPE html>
<html>
<head>
<style>
body{
  padding:10px;
  width:400px;
  margin:0 auto;
}
```

```
h1{
    text-align: center;
}
em{
    border-bottom: 1px solid green;
}

</style>
</head>
<body>
    <h1> s tag </h1>
    <p> <s> "Do not constantly spend your time
complaining about a problem you may be having or
may be up against, focus your time toward
correcting the problem. Always remember, Time is
value!" </p></s>
    <p> <s> "The best cure for one's bad tendencies is
to see them in action in another person." </p> </s>
    <p> <q>Keep smiling, because life is a beautiful
thing and there's so much to smile about. </q></p>
</body>
</html>
```

<samp> The HTML <samp> element is used to enclose inline text that represents sample (or quoted) output from a computer program. Its content is usually rendered using the browser's default fixed-spacing font.

Example:

```
<!DOCTYPE html>
<html>
<head>
<style>
body{
    padding:10px;
    width:400px;
    margin:0 auto;
}
h1{
    text-align: center;
}
```

```
em{
  border-bottom: 1px solid green;
}

</style>
</head>
<body>
  <h1> samp tag </h1>
  <p>I was trying to reboot my system, but I got
this message:</p>

  <p><samp>Keyboard not found <br>Press F1 to
continue</samp></p>
  </body>
</html>
```

<small> The HTML <small> element represents side comments and fine print, such as copyright and legal text, independent of its stylized presentation. By default, it renders the text in it one font smaller, for example from small to x-small.

<span> The HTML <span> element is an inline container for phrasing content that doesn't actually represent anything. It can use to group elements for styling elements (use the class or id attributes), or the attribute values such as lang. It should be used when no other semantic element is suitable. <span> element is very similar to the div element, but the div element is a block-level element, while the <span> element is an inline element.

Example:

```
<!DOCTYPE html>
<html>
<head>
<style>
body{
  padding:10px;
  width:400px;
  margin:0 auto;
}
h1{
```

```
      text-align: center;
    }
    em{
      border-bottom: 1px solid green;
    }
    .language{
      color:red;
      font-size:20px
    }

    </style>
    </head>
    <body>
      <h1> span tag  </h1>
      <p> There are various programming languages
  such as
        <span class="language">  Python  </span>,
        <span class="language"> Java </span>,
        <span class="language"> JavaScript </span>,
        <span class="language"> Swift </span>,
        <span class="language"> C </span> etc.
      </p>
    </body>
    </html>
```

<strong> The HTML <strong> element indicates that its content is of great importance, severity, or urgency. Browsers usually render content in bold.

Example:

```
    <!DOCTYPE html>
    <html>
    <head>
    <style>
    body{
      padding:10px;
      width:400px;
      margin:0 auto;
    }
    h1{
```

```
      text-align: center;
    }
    em{
      border-bottom: 1px solid green;
    }
    .language{
      color:red;
      font-size:20px
    }

    </style>
    </head>
    <body>
      <h1> strong tag  </h1>
      <p>Normal Text - There are various programming
languages such as Python, Java, JavaScript, Swift,
C etc. </p>
      <strong> Strong Text - There are various
programming languages such as Python, Java,
JavaScript, Swift, C etc. </strong>
    </body>
    </html>
```

<sub> The HTML <sub> element specifies embedded text that should be displayed as a subscript for typographical reasons only. Subscripts are usually rendered with a reduced outline using smaller text.

Example:

```
<!DOCTYPE html>
<html>
<head>
<style>
body{
  padding:10px;
  width:400px;
  margin:0 auto;
}
h1{
  text-align: center;
}
```

```
em{
  border-bottom: 1px solid green;
}
.language{
  color:red;
  font-size:20px
}

</style>
</head>
<body>
  <h1> sub tag  </h1>
  <p> Sub Script : H <sub> 2 </sub> O </p>
</body>
</html>
```

<sup> The HTML <sup> element specifies embedded text to be displayed as a superscript for typographical reasons only. Superscripts are usually rendered with a raised outline using smaller text.

Example:

```
<!DOCTYPE html>
<html>
<head>
<style>
body{
  padding:10px;
  width:400px;
  margin:0 auto;
}
h1{
  text-align: center;
}
em{
  border-bottom: 1px solid green;
}
.language{
  color:red;
  font-size:20px
}
```

```
</style>
</head>
<body>
  <h1> sup tag  </h1>
  <p> Super Script: (a+b) <sup> 2 </sup> </p>
</body>
</html>
```

<time> The HTML <time> element used to represent a specific time period. It can include a DateTime attribute to convert the data into a machine-readable format, allowing for search engine results or custom features such as reminders.

Example:

```
<!DOCTYPE html>
<html>
<head>
<style>
body{
  padding:10px;
  width:400px;
  margin:0 auto;
}
h1{
  text-align: center;
}
em{
  border-bottom: 1px solid green;
}
.language{
  color:red;
  font-size:20px
}

</style>
</head>
<body>
  <h1> time tag  </h1>
  <p>We will be celebrating our 40th anniversary
on <time datetime="2018-07-07">July 7</time> in
London's Hyde Park.</p>
```

```
    <p>The concert starts at <time
datetime="20:00">20:00</time> and you'll be able
to enjoy the band for at least <time
datetime="PT2H30M">2h 30m</time>.</p>
    </body>
    </html>
```

<u> The HTML <u> element represents a range of inline text that should be rendered in a way that indicates it contains non-textual annotation. This is rendered as a simple solid underline by default but can be changed with CSS.

Example:

```
<!DOCTYPE html>
<html>
<head>
<style>
body{
    padding:10px;
    width:400px;
    margin:0 auto;
}
h1{
    text-align: center;
}
em{
    border-bottom: 1px solid green;
}
.language{
    color:red;
    font-size:20px
}

</style>
</head>
<body>
    <h1> strong tag  </h1>
    <p> Normal Text - There are various
programming languages such as Python, Java,
JavaScript, Swift, C etc. </p>
```

```
    <u> Underline Text - There are various
programming languages such as Python, Java,
JavaScript, Swift, C etc. </u>
    </body>
    </html>
```

<var> The HTML <var> element represents the name of a variable in a mathematical expression or in a programming context. It usually displays the current version of the font in italics, although this behavior depends on the browser.

Example:

```
<!DOCTYPE html>
<html>
<head>
<style>
body{
    padding:10px;
    width:400px;
    margin:0 auto;
}
h1{
    text-align: center;
}
em{
    border-bottom: 1px solid green;
}
.language{
    color:red;
    font-size:20px
}

</style>
</head>
<body>
    <h1> strong tag </h1>
    <p> The area of a triangle can be calculated
with the help of the formula: A = 1/2 ( <var> b </
var> x <var> h </var>)</p>
    <p>The volume of a box is <var>l</var> x
<var>w</var> x <var>h</var>, where <var>l</var>
```

represents the length, `<var>w</var>` the width and
`<var>h</var>` the height of the box.`</p>`
`<p>` The perimeter P of a rectangle is given by
the formula, P=2`<var>` l `</var>` + 2 `<var>w</var>`,
where l is the length and w is the width of the
rectangle. `</p>`
`<p>` The area A of a rectangle is given by the
formula, A= `<var>` l `</var>` `<var>` w `</var>`, where
`<var>` l `</var>` is the length and `<var>` w `</var>` is
the width. `</p>`
`</body>`
`</html>`

`<wbr>` The HTML `<wbr>` element represents a word break opportunity –
a position within text where the browser may break a line, though the line-
breaking rules would not otherwise create a break at that location.

Example:

```
<!DOCTYPE html>
<html>
<head>
<style>
body{
  padding:10px;
  width:400px;
  margin:0 auto;
}
h1{
  text-align: center;
}

#example-paragraphs {
    background-color: grey;
    overflow: hidden;
    resize: horizontal;
    width: 9rem;
}

  </style>
  </head>
  <body>
```

```
<h1> wbr tag  </h1>
<div id="example-paragraphs">
    <p>Sed varius elit eget diam cursus
tincidunt. Donec sagittis vehicula neque, sit amet
accumsan massa imperdiet a. Maecenas vel nunc sed
nibh lacinia pulvinar.
       Morbi aliquet massa a ipsum sodales, vel
aliquam arcu viverra.</p>
    <p> Maecenas vel nunc <wbr>sed<wbr>nibh
<wbr>lacinia<wbr>gesetz</p>
  </div>   </body>
  </html>
```

IMAGE AND MULTIMEDIA

HTML supports a variety of multimedia resources such as images, audio, and videos.[3]

- <area> The HTML <area> element defines an area inside an image map that has predefined clickable areas. An image map allows geometric regions in an image to be hyperlinked.

- <audio> The HTML <audio> element is used to add audio content to documents. It can contain one or more audio sources, represented by the src attribute or the source element: the browser selects the most appropriate one. It can also be a target for streaming media using MediaStream.

- <img> The HTML <img> element inserts an image into a document.

- <map> The HTML <map> element is always used with <area> elements to define an image map (clickable area of a link).

- <track> The HTML <track> element helps as a child of media elements, audio, and videos. Allows you to specify timed text tracks (or time-based data), for example for automatic subtitle processing. These tracks are formatted in (.vtt files) WebVTT format that is Web Video Text Tracks.

- <video> The HTML <video> element used to embed a media player in the document that supports video playback. You can use <video> for audio content, but an audio element may provide a more appropriate user experience.

ELEMENT DESCRIPTION

In addition to normal multimedia content, HTML can contain a variety of other content, although it is not always easy to work with it.[4]

- <embed> The HTML <embed> element used to embed external content at a specified location in the document. The content is provided by an external application or other source of content, such as a browser plug-in.

- <iframe> The HTML <iframe> element defines a nested browsing context that inserts another HTML page into the current page.

- <object> The HTML <object> element represents an external resource that can be treated as an image, browsing nested context, or a resource to be handled by a plugin.

- <picture> The HTML <picture> element contains zero or more source elements and one img element that offers alternative versions of the image for different display/device scenarios.

- <portal> The HTML <portal> element allows you to insert another HTML page into the current page to allow smoother navigation to new pages.

- <source> The HTML <source> element specifies various media sources for an image, audio element, or video element. It is an empty element, meaning it has no content and no closing tag. It is used to offer the same media content in multiple file formats to ensure compatibility with a wide range of browsers due to their different support for image file formats and media file formats.

SVG AND MathML

You can embed SVG and MathML content into the HTML documents using the <svg> and <math> elements.

<svg> The HTML <svg> element is a container that defines a coordinate system and viewport. It is used as the outer-most element of documents, but can also be used to insert an SVG fragment into an SVG or HTML document.

<math> The top-level HTML element in MathML is <math>. Every valid instance of MathML must be wrapped in <math> tags. Additionally,

you cannot nest a second <math> element inside another element, but you can have any number of other child elements within it.

SCRIPTING

In order to create dynamic web applications, HTML supports the use of scripting languages, primarily JavaScript. Some elements support this ability.

<canvas> Use the HTML <canvas> element with the canvas scripting API or the WebGL API to draw graphics and animations.

<noscript> The HTML <noscript> element defines the part of HTML to be inserted if the script type is not supported on the page or if scripting is currently disabled in the browser.

<script> The HTML <script> element is used to insert executable code or data; this is typically used to embed or reference JavaScript code. The <script> element can be used with other languages such as the WebGL shader GLSL programming language and JSON.

TEXT ALTERATION

These elements allow you to provide indications that certain parts of the text have been changed.

<del> The HTML <del> element defines a range of text that has been removed from a document. This can be used, for example, when plotting "tracking changes" or information about source code differences. The HTML <ins> element can use for the different purposes to indicate text that has been added to the document.

<ins> This element represents a range of text added to a document. You can use the del element to same represent a range of text that has been removed from a document.

TABLE CONTENTS

The elements are used to create and process tabular data.

- <caption> The HTML <caption> element specifies the caption (or heading) of the table.

- <col> The HTML <col> element defines a column in a table and is used to define common semantics for all common cells. It is usually found in the colgroup element.

- <colgroup> The HTML <colgroup> element represents a group of columns in a table.

- <table> The HTML <table> element represents tabular data that information presented in a two-dimensional table composed of rows and columns of cells containing data.

- <tbody> The HTML <tbody> element encapsulates a set of table rows (tr elements), which means it forms the body of the <table> (table).

- <td> The HTML <td> element defines a table cell that contains data. It participates in the tabular model.

- <tfoot> The HTML <tfoot> element represents a set of rows summarizing table columns.

- <th> The HTML <th> element represents a cell as the header of a group of table cells. The exact nature group is defined by the scope and headers attribute.

- <thead> The HTML <thead> element represents a set of lines defining table column headers.

- <tr> The HTML <tr> element is used to represent a row of cells in a table. Row cells can then be created using a combination of td (table data cell) and th (table header cell) elements.

FORMS CONTENT

HTML language provides a number of elements that can be used together to create forms that a user can fill and submit to a web page or application. Much more information about this is available in the HTML form guide.

- <button> The HTML <button> element is an interactive element activated by the user using a mouse, keyboard, finger, command, or other assistive technology. Once activated, it will then perform a programmable action, such as submitting a form or opening a dialog.

- <datalist> The HTML <datalist> element consists a set of option elements that represent the allowed or recommended options available for selection within other controls.

- <fieldset> The HTML <fieldset> element is used to control and label within a web form.

- <form> The HTML <form> element defines a section of a document containing interactive controls for submitting information.

- <input> The HTML <input> element helps to create controls for web forms to accept data from the user; a wide variety of input data types and control widgets are depending on the device and user agent. The <input> element is powerful and complex in all of HTML due to the huge number of combinations of input types and attributes.

- <label> The HTML <label> element represents a label for an item in the user interface.

- <legend> The HTML <legend> element used to define a caption for the content of its parent fieldset.

- <meter> The HTML <meter> element defines either a scalar value in a known range or a fractional value.

- <optgroup> The HTML <optgroup> element helps to create a grouping of options within the <select> element.

- <option> The HTML <option> element is used to define an item that contains a select, optgroup, or datalist element. The <option> element can represent menu items in pop-ups and other item lists in an HTML document.

- <output> The HTML <output> element is a container element into which a website or application can insert the results of a calculation or the result of a user action.

- <progress> The HTML <progress> element shows an indicator that shows the progress of a task's completion, usually displayed as a progress bar.

- <select> The HTML <select> element defines a control that provides a menu of options.

- <textarea> The HTML <textarea> element is a multiline plain text editing control that is useful when you want to allow users to enter large amounts of free-form text, such as a review comment or feedback form.

OTHER INTERACTIVE ELEMENTS

HTML offers a selection of elements that help create interactive user interface objects.

<details> The HTML <details> element creates an accessibility widget in which information is only visible when the widget is switched to the "open" state. A label must be provided using the details element.

<dialog> The HTML <dialog> element represents a dialog box or other component, such as a dismissable alert, inspector, or pane.

<summary> The HTML <summary> element specifies a summary, title, or legend for the disclosure field of the detail element. Clicking on the <summary> element toggles the open and closed state of the parent <details> element.

WEB COMPONENTS

Web Components is a technology related to HTML that basically allows you to create custom elements as if it was regular HTML. You can create your versions of standard HTML elements.

<slot> The HTML <slot> element – part of the Web Components suite of technologies – is a placeholder inside a component that you can fill with your own markup, allowing you to create separate Document Object Model (DOM) trees and present them together.

<template> The HTML <template> element is a way for holding HTML that is not meant to be rendered immediately after page load but can be instantiated later at runtime using JavaScript.

INLINE VS. BLOCK ELEMENTS

Block-Level Elements

HTML elements have historically been categorized as either block-level elements or inline-level elements. Since this is a presentational characteristic, nowadays CSS is specified in Flow Layout. A block-level element gets the entire horizontal space of its parent element (that is called as a container) and space equals to the height of its content, creating a "block".

The following is a list of all block-level HTML elements (although the word block-level is not defined for elements that are new to HTML5).

- <address>: It is used to contact information.

- <article>: It defines content of the article.

- <aside>: It is content aside.

- <blockquote>: It is a long ("block") quote.

- <details>: It is a publish widget.

- <dialog>: It is a dialog window.

- <dd>: It describes a term in the list of descriptions.

- <div>: It is used to distribute documents.

- <dl>: It is a descriptive list.

- <dt>: It is a descriptive list term.

- <fieldset>: It is a field set label.

- <figcaption>: It is a description of the picture.

- <image>: It defines the groups media content with a caption (see <figcaption>).

- <footer>: It is the footer of a section or page.

- <form>: It is an entry form.

- <h1>, <h2>, <h3>, <h4>, <h5>, <h6>: It is heading Levels 1–6.

- <header>: It is a section or page header.

- <hgroup>: It is a group header information.

- <game>: It is the horizontal ruler (dividing line).

- <li>: It defines list item.

- <main>: It contains central content unique to this document.

- <nav>: It contains navigation links.

- <ol>: It is an ordered list.

- <p>: It is a paragraph.

- <before>: It is used to preformatted text.

- <section>: It defines the part of a website.

- <table>: It is a table.

- <ul>: It is an unordered list.

Inline elements: Inline elements only take up enough width to allow for other elements next to each other that are inline. Inline elements do not start on a fresh line and do not have top and bottom borders like block elements. Examples of embedded elements:

- <a>: This tag is used to include hyperlinks on a web page.

-
: This tag is used to mention line breaks on a web page whenever needed.

- <script>: This tag is used to include external and internal JavaScript codes.

- <input>: This tag is used to receive input from users and is mainly used in forms.

- <img>: This tag is used to include various images on a web page to make the page look beautiful.

- <span>: This tag is an inline container that takes up only the necessary space.

- <b>: This tag is used where bold text is needed.

- <label>: This tag is used to improve usability for mouse users, i.e. if the user clicks on the text in the <label> element, it toggles the control.

ANATOMY OF HTML ELEMENTS

It is the global structure of an HTML that includes HTML version, HTML elements, attributes, inline and block elements, editors, formatting, and paragraphs.[5] As more and more editors are expected to proofread content on the web, it's increasingly helpful for us to know at least the basics of HTML. So here is a simple introduction to the web language.

Whenever you view a web page, your web browser converts the HTML code into rendered text, images, and other media. If you ever want to fix or modify the content of the page, you will often need to change this HTML code. The very thought of it strikes fear into many hearts, but it doesn't have to.

- Elements the building blocks of HTML

- Creating an HTML document

- Building the hierarchy of HTML

- Paragraphs and formatting

- Image

- Listing

- Links

- Heading

- Comments

- Tables

- Special characters

- And more

HTML is made of a series of hierarchal elements. Most elements have an opening and closing tag, with some content in between. If you are used to mark up chapters, headings, and subheadings, this concept should be easy to grasp. Here's an example of the <p> paragraph element:

```
<p> Define Paragraph: The content of paragraph goes
between the opening and closing tags. The block will
be treated as a single paragraph with block content
element.</p>.
```

A small number of elements use a single tag. These are referred to as self-closing elements. Here's an instance of a self-closing element – the line break (<br>).

```
Define <br/>: The line breaks insert new lines into
<br>
the text. It is good to <br>
use paragraph elements instead of <br> tag.
```

Creating an HTML Document

With a fundamental understanding of the sorts of elements that exist, we can start to build an HTML page. First, let's create the file that contains our code:

- Create a new text file in any plain-text editor such as Notepad in (Windows) or TextEdit in (Mac).

- Then save the empty file as sample.html (.html is an extension).

- We recommend you to use any text editor to write code in HTML.

OK, we now save the file somewhere to place HTML code. When you are done editing the sample file, we can save the file, close it, and then double-click to reopen it in a web browser (by default, the .html files open by own in a web browser).

The simplest documents start with this opening tag such as

```
<html>
```

We can show our data correctly on the web browsers by declaring the HTML standard. To use the latest HTML5 standard, you should start our book as follows:

```
<!DOCTYPE html>
</html>
```

Because <html> is a standard element, it should have an opening tag and a closing tag. Therefore, at the end of the source code, we'll use this code:

```
<!DOCTYPE html>
<html>
<head> </head>
<body> </body>
</html>
```

Let's put this together and see what we will get:

```
<!DOCTYPE html>
<html>
<head> </head>
<body> </body>
</html>
```

CREATING THE HIERARCHY OF HTML

Just as a branch of the tree, the elements in HTML can be nested within other elements. Our root <html> element must be contained the following elements, in the same order such as:

- <head> – it includes information about the page
- <body> – it includes information displayed on the page

The code defines a basic, empty HTML page. Anything we add to the page will be nested within the <head> or <body> elements. These elements will become the parents of their child elements.

PAGE TITLES

We can add a title to the page by including a <title> tag within the <head> element also its closing tag. Here's how that looks given below.

```
<head>
    <title> Here the page title goes </title>
    </head>
```

In HTML, you can add spaces and tabs that return it anywhere, and the code will still work.

You won't see the page title appears in the main part of the web browser screen, but it's often displayed at the very top of the browser window on the new Tab.

PARAGRAPHS AND FORMATTING

Most text on the page should be placed inside the block element tag <p> tags within the <body> element. We can usually set text in bold or italics by using the <strong> and <em> elements respectively. Here's an example such as,

```
<html>
<head>
<title> </title>
</head>
<body>
```

```
<p> It is text sits within a paragraph element.</p>
<p> the other elements are used to write text in
<strong> bold </strong> or
<em> It is new tag to write your text in italics as
(<i>) tag </em>.</p>
</body>
</html>
```

HEADINGS

HTML supports six levels of heading. Here's the code you'll need such as,

```
<!DOCTYPE html>
<html lang="en">
<head>
    <meta charset="UTF-8">
    <meta HTTP-equiv="X-UA-Compatible"
content="IE=edge">
    <meta name="viewport" content="width=device-width,
initial-scale=1.0"  name="viewport" >
    <title>Document</title>
</head>
<body>
    <h1> This is a level first heading </h1>
<h2> This is a level second heading </h2>
<h3> This is a level third  heading< /h3>
<h4> This is a level fourth heading </h4>
<h5> This is a level fifth heading </h5>
<h6> This is a level sixth heading </h6>

</body>
</html>
```

The level 1 heading (<h1>) is the upper level on the page. It appears at or near the top of the page, and it is good to use just one <h1> on each page. It is for an <h2> to be used after an <h1>, for an <h3> to be used after an <h2>, and so on.

IMAGES

Images are added by using the self-closing tag <img> element. We use 'attributes' inside the element to specify an image to display and to provide information about the image. Here is an example of an <img> element with 3 attributes. Here is an example of an <img> element with three attributes:

Example:

```
<img src="https://images.pexels.com/photos/12586694/
pexels-photo-12586694.jpeg?auto=compress&cs=tinysrgb
&w=300&lazy=load" alt="Flower" title="Flower">
```

Let's look at each part of the code:

- <img> – It is an element used to display an image.

- src="" – It is an attribute used to set the name and location of the image file.

- alt="" – It is an attribute used to set the text to display when the image can't be loaded.

- title="" – It is an attribute used to set the text to display when the pointer hovers over the image.

Image Sources

The src="…" attribute has to be written so that the image can be located. It is important to know how to locate the image on your website otherwise it won't end up with a broken image on your page.

There are various ways to define the correct 'path' to an image. You can find the easiest method to start from the top level of the web server and list every folder that has to be opened to reach the image.

Here's an example: let's say that we give online URL of flower photo from pexels.com (you can copy the img source address by right-clicking and pasting in the src of the img tag). You can add your local file image just by finding the path of it.

Example:

```
<html>
<head>
<title> </title>
</head>
```

```
<body>
<p> Image (using url) </p>
<img src="https://images.pexels.com/
photos/12586694/pexels-photo-12586694.jpeg?auto=co
mpress&cs=tinysrgb&w=300&lazy=load" alt="Flower"
title="Flower">
</body>
</html>
```

LINKS

If you want to link from one page to another, we use the <a> element (it stands for 'anchor'). It takes an href="..." attribute, which is used to specify the address of the destination page.

```
<a href="https://www.google.com/"> Search anything
using google </a>
```

Note: A closing </a> tags the text between the tags is what turns into the familiar, clickable hyperlink.

It is useful attributes of anchor links:

- title="..." – the text that appears by hovering over the link.

- target="..." – use target="_blank" to force the link to open in a new browser window

LISTS

HTML supports these list types:[6]

- Unordered (<ul>) – It is bulleted lists

- Ordered (<ol>) – It is numbered lists

Unordered Lists

An ordered list is created using the <ol> element. All list items within are created using the <li> element.

Ordered lists are used when the list items should follow a sequence, with normal numerals (1, 2, 3, etc.) as the default list item markers.

The individual entries in each type of list are created with the <li> ('list item') element. Here's an example of an unordered list given below.

Example:

```
<html>
<head>
<title> Title </title>
</head>
<body>
<ul>
    <li> HTML </li>
    <li> CSS </li>
    <li> PHP </li>
</ul>
</body>
</html>
```

Here's the browser output of this unordered list:

1. HTML

2. CSS

3. PHP

Ordered Lists

An ordered list is created using the <ol> element. All list items within are created using the <li> element.

Ordered lists are used when the list items should follow a sequence, with normal numerals (1, 2, 3, etc.) as the default list item markers.

```
<html>
<head>
<title> Title </title>
</head>
<body>
<ul>
    <ol> HTML </ol>
    <ol> CSS </ol>
    <ol> PHP </ol>
</ul>
</body>
</html>
```

Here's the browser output of this unordered list:

1. HTML

2. CSS

3. PHP

ANOTHER WAY TO LIST STYLES

It is special list styles that allow us to use alternative numbering schemes. Here is an example:

```
<html>
<head>
<title> Title </title>
</head>
<body>
<ol style="list-style-type:lower-roman;">
    <li> HTML </li>
    <li> CSS /li>
    <li> PHP /li>
</ol>
</body>
</html>
```

You can add your list style inline the <ol> and <ul> tags. If you want to change the list numbers themselves (rather than just their style), you can do this by using the start="n" attribute on the <ol> element, where *n* represents the number at which the list should start.

```
<html>
    <head>
    <title> Title </title>
    </head>
    <body>
    <h2> Normal List with starting numbering </h1>
    <ol>
        <li> First step </li>
        <li> Second step </li>
    </ol>
```

```
Here some text that breaks up the list.
  <!-- Thebreak in the list can be of any length. -->

<h2> Normal List with restarting numbering from 3
number </h1>
  <ol start="3">
     <li> Third step </li>
     <li> Fourth step </li>
  </ol>
  </body>
  </html>
```

And here's the result of the following code:

1. First step

2. Second step

3. Third step

4. Fourth step

Another approach is to use the value="n" attribute on the same <li> element. Here, *n* represents the number to assign to the targeted <li> element.

Example:

```
<html>
<head>
<title> Title </title>
</head>
<body>
<h2> Normal List with starting numbering </h1>
<ol>
   <li> First step </li>
   <li> Second step </li>
   <li value="3"> Third step </li> <!-- The number
adjust automatically -->
   <li value="4"> Fourth step </li>
</ol>
</body>
```

REVERSE-ORDERED LISTS

The reversed allows to reverse the ordering of ordered lists, which can be useful for creating a countdown.

```
<html>
<head>
<title> Title </title>
</head>
<body>
<h2> Normal List with reversed numbering </h1>
    <ol reversed>
        <li> HTML  </li> <!-- It could be numbered
3 -->
        <li> CSS </li> <!-- It could be numbered 2 -->
        <li> PHP </li>   <!-- It could be numbered
1 -->
    </ol>

</body>
```

LIST STYLE TYPE

Here are various list style types:

- circle

- square

- upper-roman

- lower-alpha

Example:

```
<!DOCTYPE html>
<html>
<head>
<title> Title </title>
</head>
<body>
<h1>The list-style-type Property</h1>
<p> Example of unordered lists:</p>
```

```
<ul style="list-style-type: circle">
    <li> HTML </li>
    <li> CSS /li>
    <li> PHP /li>
</ul>

<ul style="list-style-type: square">
    <li> HTML </li>
    <li> CSS /li>
    <li> PHP /li>
</ul>

<p>Example of ordered lists:</p>
<ol style="list-style-type:  lower-alpha">
    <li> HTML </li>
    <li> CSS /li>
    <li> PHP /li>
</ol>

<ol style="list-style-type:  upper-roman">
    <li> HTML </li>
    <li> CSS /li>
    <li> PHP /li>
</ol>

</body>
</html>
```

MULTILEVEL LISTS

If you need to create lists inside another list, place the code for a list inside the item list of a parent list.

Example:

```
<!DOCTYPE html>
<html>
<head>
<title> Title </title>
</head>
<body>
<ul class="bullet">
```

```
        <li>Programming Languages
            <ul class="bullet">
                <li>  HTML </li>
                <li> CSS </li>
            </ul>
        </li>
        <li> PHP </li>
        <li> Python </li>
    </ul>
    </body>
    </html>
```

COMMENTS

HTML allows us to write comments in code. The comments are useful for leaving notes about what certain pieces of code do. The comments are not displayed when the page appears in a browser, but they can be viewed who look at the page source using Ctrl + u. Comments start & end with <!-- and - -> tags. In the following code example, the comment is shown.

```
<html>
<head> <title> </title></head>
<body>
<!-- This is a heading tag -->
<h1> You are learning HTML </h1>
<!-- This is a paragraph tag -->
<p> Here is an introductory paragraph. </p>
</body>
```

TABLES

We use tables to display information that is presented in tabular form. The common use of tables is to control the layout of a page.

Most of the tables are made up of the following elements:

- <table> – the element contains all information about the table.

- <tr> – the 'table row' element defines a row.

- <th> – the 'table heading' element defines a heading cell.

- <td> – the 'table data' element defines a cell.

- The <table> element should appear within the document's <body> element.

Example:

```
<html>
<head>
<title> Title <title>
 </head>
<body>
<!-- Some elements could appear here -->
<table>
    <tr>  <!-- Beginning of the 1st row -->
        <th> Row 1, column 1 </th> <!-- 1st
heading cell in this row -->
        <th> Row 1, column 2</th> <!-- 2nd heading
cell in this row -->
    </tr> <!-- End of the 1st row -->
    <tr>
        <td> Row 2, column 1 </td>
        <td> Row 2, column 2 </td>
    </tr>
    <tr>  <!-- Beginning of the 3rd row -->
        <td> Row 3, column 1 </td> <!-- 1st data
cell in this row -->
        <td>Row 3, column 2</td> <!-- 2nd data
cell in this row -->
    </tr>   <!-- End of the 3rd row -->
    <tr>
        <td> Row 4, column 1 </td>
        <td> Row 4, column 2 </td>
    </tr>
</table>
</body>
</html>
```

There are various attributes supported by the table. The <table> tag supports its own set of attributes, with three of the commonest ones shown in this example:

```
<table border="1" cellpadding="5" cellspacing="10">
    <!-- Here will be your rest of the code within the
table -->
    </table>
```

Here's what these attributes do:

- border – It defines the width in pixels of the border around the table.

- cellpadding – It defines the space in pixels between the cell content and the cell.

- cellspacing – It defines the space in pixels between cells.

SPECIAL CHARACTERS

If you write content for the web, it is good to use characters that are not labeled on most keyboards.

Serial	Term	Character	Entity	Numeric
1	Ampersand	&	&amp;	&#38;
2	Non-breaking space			
3	Pound	£	&pound;	&#163;
4	Copyright	©	&copy;	&#169;
5	Registered trademark	®	&reg;	&#174;
6	Degrees	°	&deg;	&#176;
7	Lowercase acute	é	&eacute;	&#233;
8	En dash	–	&ndash;	&#8211;
9	Em dash	—	&mdash;	&#8212;
10	Left single quote	'	&lsquo;	&#8216;
11	Right single quote	'	&rsquo;	&#8217;
12	Left double quote	"	&ldquo;	&#8220;
13	Right double quote	"	&rdquo;	&#8221;

BLOCKQUOTES

The <blockquote> element sets content apart from the copy above and below. It gives us a good way to display quotations and other notes. Here's an example of the <blockquote> element given below.

```
<!DOCTYPE html>
<html lang="en">
```

```
<head>
    <meta charset="UTF-8">
    <meta HTTP-equiv="X-UA-Compatible"
content="IE=edge">
    <meta content="width=device-width, initial-
scale=1.0"> name="viewport"
    <title>Document</title>
</head>
<body>
    <p>This is a normal paragraph.</p>
<blockquote> <p> This text has been placed into a
blockquote element to show that happens when using
basic quoting features in HTML. All browsers handle
blockquotes differently, but the general behaviour
is pretty much the same across the board. </p>
</blockquote>

</body>
</html>
```

In the blockquotes, you will get your content with a little bit of space from the left side in the output

CHAPTER SUMMARY

In this chapter, beginners will get knowledge of basic structure of HTML and various elements of HTML with categories. In the next chapter, we will discuss text formatting and links in HTML.

NOTES

1. HTML Structure – https://developer.mozilla.org/en-US/docs/Learn/Getting_started_with_the_web/HTML_basics#anatomy_of_an_html_element, accessed on August 4, 2022.
2. HTML Elements References – https://developer.mozilla.org/en-US/docs/Web/HTML/Element#content_sectioning, accessed on August 4, 2022.
3. HTML Elements References – https://developer.mozilla.org/en-US/docs/Web/HTML/Element#content_sectioning, accessed on August 4, 2022.
4. Element Content – https://developer.mozilla.org/en-US/docs/Web/HTML/Element#image_and_multimedia, accessed on August 5, 2022.
5. Anatomy of HTML Elements https://espirian.co.uk/anatomy-of-an-html-page/#elements, accessed on August 8, 2022.
6. List – https://espirian.co.uk/anatomy-of-an-html-page/, accessed on August 8, 2022.

Elements and Its Attributes

The previous chapter was all about the structure of HTML. Here we will learn elements and attributes. Before starting the discussion of HTML elements attributes, let's discuss the difference between the tags and elements.

In HTML, tags are used at the start and end of an element. The element itself consists of tags and a structure inside. And attributes are given to elements to define their properties. Hopefully, this will provide you with a better understanding of tags, elements, and attributes.

HTML TAGS

Tags are used to define the start and end of an HTML element.[1] They consist of an opening parenthesis (<) followed by the name of the element and then a closing parenthesis (>). If an attribute is used in the

DOI: 10.1201/9781003358077-3

tag, it will be placed after the element. Here is an example of the HTML title tag.

```
<title> <title>
```

HTML ELEMENTS

An element contains opening and closing tags, as well as what's inside those tags.[2] It usually consists of some structure that is used to define the relevant tags. Here is an example of an HTML title element.

Syntax:

```
<tagname> your content goes </tagname>
```

The HTML element is the start tag to the end tag.

Example:

```
<title> My Website </title>
```

In this example, the HTML element is the heading "My Website" complete with opening and closing title tags. An element is defined by a start and end tag, some content, and an end tag.

The browser is the main tool of the web. So you should have a working knowledge of HTML5 and CSS3 programming because all your users are viewing your site using one browser or the other.

WEB BROWSERS

A web browser is a software application that is for the purpose of reading instructions and displaying the result on the web page.[3] It is fully functional software that can interpret and display HTML of web pages, applications, JavaScript, AJAX, and others hosted on web servers. HTML is responsible for telling the web browser how text and other objects in a web document should appear. The Hypertext Transfer Protocol (HTTP) defines how browsers should request web pages and how web servers should respond to those requests.

How Does It Work?

A web browser typically reads and renders HTML documents. This happens inside the browser in two phases – the parsing phase and the rendering phase. During the parsing phase, the browser reads the markup in the document, breaks it down into components, and creates a Document Object Model (DOM). After creating the DOM tree and loading and parsing all CSS stylesheets, the browser starts the rendering phase. Each node in the DOM tree will be rendered and displayed in the browser.

HTML Web Browser Support

All web activity begins on the user side when a user launches their browser. Each browser renders HTML a little differently, for example, handles JavaScript, multimedia, stylesheets, and other HTML plugins differently. Web browsers were created specifically to read HTML instructions and display the resulting web page. So when you're working with HTML, you need to test your site in as many different browsers as possible.

The purpose of a browser such as Chrome, Edge, Firefox, Safari is to read documents and display them correctly.[4] The browser does not display HTML tags, uses them to determine how to display the document.

1. **Internet Explorer:** Microsoft Internet Explorer (IE) remains the dominant player on the Internet. Explorer is still very popular because it comes with Microsoft Windows. Of course, it works exclusively with Microsoft Windows. Mac and Linux are not supported. Version 10 of IE finally has respectable major parts of the HTML5 standard. If you write pages according to the HTML5 version, you can expect your site to work well in IE10. Most features will work in IE9, but not all.

   But the older versions of IE are still extremely important because so many computers don't have IE10 installed yet. Version 6 has been the dominant player on the Internet for some time and refuses to die. However, it won't play well with modern standards, so it's considered obsolete by most developers.

2. **Mozilla Firefox:** Firefox is a big improvement on IE from a programmer's perspective due to the following reasons:

   • Better code display: If you view the HTML code of the page, you will see the code in a special window. The code has syntax coloring, making it easy to read. Some versions of IE display the code in Notepad, which is confusing because if you think you can edit the code, but you are simply editing the copy.

- Better error handling: You will make mistakes. In general, Firefox is better at pointing out errors than IE, especially when you start using JavaScript and other advanced technologies.

- Great extensions: Firefox has some amazing extensions that make web development a lot easier. These extensions allow you to edit code on the fly, automatically validate code, and dynamically examine your page structure.

- Cross-platform support: IE only works on Windows operating system, so it is not available for Mac or Linux users. Even if you are a Windows-only developer, your users might be using something else, so you need to know how other browsers see things.

3. **Safari:** The default browser for Mac and iPhone/iPad operating system (iOS) is called Safari. It is a powerful browser built on the WebKit rendering engine. Safari was designed with compliance and speed in mind. Mac and iOS users will certainly be using Safari, so you should know something about it. Chrome also uses WebKit, so if it looks good in Chrome, you'll probably be fine with Apple users.

4. **Google Chrome:** Google sees the future of browser-based applications using AJAX technologies. The Chrome is extremely fast, especially in the JavaScript technology that serves as the basis of this strategy. Chrome has a number of developer tools that make it the browser of choice for many web developers. Here are the highlights.

   - Real-time edits: You can go to any web page, right-click "inspect this element" and edit the text of that element in real-time. You can then see how the element looks with the new content. You can select a part of the page to see which corresponds to the code; you can select a code to see which part of the page the code represents.

   - Page outline: A well-designed page is created in the form of an outline with various elements nested within each other. The Elements View allows you to view a web page in the format with the ability to collapse and expand elements to clearly see the structure of the page.

   - Real-time CSS edits: As you learn how to use CSS styles, you'll want to see how different CSS rules change your page. In the

Explore Element view, you can highlight a part of the page and change the CSS while watching how the change affects your page in real-time.

- Network Tab feature allows user to see how long each part of your page takes to load. This can be useful when troubleshooting a slow-loading page.
- View sources: It allows you to view the full code of your page. It's especially useful when you get into JavaScript programming, as it includes a powerful debugging suite.
- Console: The console view is a small command line tool integrated directly into your browser. This can be very useful as it often shows errors that are otherwise hidden. The console is most useful when using JavaScript.

HTML ATTRIBUTES

Some characters are reserved in HTML.[5] If you use the symbol less than (<) or greater than (>) signs in any text, the browser mixes them with tags.

Character entities are used to show reserved characters in HTML. A character entity looks like this:

```
&entity_name;
```

OR

```
&#entity_number;
```

NON-BREAKING SPACE

A commonly used entity in HTML is the non-breaking space: a non-breaking space that will not break into a new line.[6] The two words separated by a non-breaking space will stick together (not break into a new line).

COMBINING DIACRITICAL MARKS

A mark is a "glyph" added to a letter. Some of the diacritical marks, such as grave (`) and acute (´), are called accents. Diacritical marks can appear above and below a letter, within a letter, and between two letters.

This marks can be used in combination with alpha-numeric characters to create a character set (encoding) used on the page.

The attributes are used to define a property for more than one HTML element. They are found in the opening tag of an element and often contain spaces that are separated by pairs of values. Here is an example of the HTML alt text attribute:

```
<img src="https://images.pexels.com/photos/56866/
garden-rose-red-pink-56866.jpeg?auto=compress&cs=tinys
rgb&w=300" alt="Red pink rose">
```

In this example, the attribute is named an alt text of "Red Pink Rose" for the image "https://images.pexels.com/photos/56866/garden-rose-red-pink-56866.jpeg?auto=compress&cs=tinysrgb&w=300". While images will be rendered and displayed regardless of whether or not they contain alt text, adding this attribute is several different reasons.ood The search engines pay close attention to the alt text attribute of images, using this information to determine their meaning.

We have seen several HTML tags and their uses such as heading tags <h1>, <h2>, paragraph tag <p>, and other tags.[7] So far we've used them in their simplest form, but most HTML tags can also have attributes, which are extra bits of information.

All attributes consist of two parts – a name and a value:

- Name is the property that you want to see for getting data in database or fetch. For example, the <p> paragraph element in the example carries an attribute named align, which you can use to indicate the alignment of the paragraph on the page.

- The value is what you want the property value to be set to and is always enclosed in quotes. The following example shows three possible values for the align attribute: left, center, and right.

Attribute names and attribute values are not case sensitive. However, the World Wide Web Consortium (W3C) Organization recommends lowercase attributes/attribute values in its HTML 4 Recommendation.

```
<!DOCTYPE html>
<html>
```

```
    <head>
       <title>Align Attribute  Example</title>
    </head>
    <body>
       <p align = "left"> This text will be left
aligned </p>
       <p align = "center"> This text will be center
aligned </p>
       <p align = "right"> This text will be right
aligned </p>
    </body>
</html>
```

Core Attributes

There are four core attributes that can be used on the majority of HTML elements:

- Id
- Title
- Class
- Style

Let's discuss all one by one.

ID Attributes

The id attribute can be used to uniquely identify any element within an HTML page. There are two primary reasons that you want to use an id attribute on an element given below:

- If an element carries a unique id attribute as a unique identifier, it is easy to identify its element content.

- If you have two elements of the same name within a single page (or style sheet), you can use the unique id attribute to distinguish between elements that have the same name.

Example:

```
<html>
<head>
```

```
</head>
<body>
<p id = "HTML"> You are learning HTML </p>
<p id = "CSS"> After HTML you will learn CSS. </p>
</body>
</html>
```

The title attribute provides a suggested title for the element. The syntax for the title attribute is the same as explained for the id attribute. The behavior of the attribute will depend upon the element that carries it; however, it is displayed as a tooltip when the mouse cursor comes over the element or while the element is loading.

Example:

```
<!DOCTYPE html>
<html>
    <head>
        <title>The title Attribute Example</title>
    </head>
    <body>
        <h3 title = "HTML! "> You are learning HTML
</h3>
    </body>
</html>
```

The class Attribute
The class attribute is used to link an element with a style sheet that specifies the class of element. You will learn much more about the use of the class attribute when you will learn CSS. The value of this class attribute may be a space-separated list of class names. Here is the syntax of the class attributes.

```
class = "className1 className2 className3"
```

Example:

```
class = "row title text"
```

You can write anything in the class followed by various names.

```
<html>
<head>
```

```
 <title> Tittle </title>
</head>
<body>
<p class= "row1 html"> You are learning HTML </p>
<p class= "row1 css"> After HTML you will learn CSS.
</p>
</body>
</html>
```

The style Attribute

The style attribute allows to specify CSS rules within the element.

```
<!DOCTYPE html>
<html>
    <head>
        <title> The style Attribute </title>
    </head>
    <body>
        <p style = "font-family: arial; color: yellow;">
Write your code here ... </p>
    </body>
</html>
```

The additional values that configure the elements are listed below. HTML attributes provide additional information about HTML elements.

All elements can have attributes.[8] It provides extra information about elements. They are specified in the start tag. It usually comes in name/ value pairs like: name="value. Now we will talk about some important attributes of some of the tags below:

- The src Attribute

- The width and height Attributes

- The href Attribute

- The alt Attribute

- The style Attribute

- The lang Attribute

- The title Attribute

These attributes are frequently used by the users, but the list is too big for HTML attributes.

GLOBAL ATTRIBUTES LIST

HTML5 defines a few attributes that are common to all elements. These attributes specify all elements, such as elements found inside the <head> section of the document, e.g. <base>, <script>, <title> etc.

Attribute	Value	Description
accesskey	shortcut key	It specifies a keyboard shortcut to activate or focus the element.
class	class name	It assigns a class name or space-separated list of class names to an element.
contenteditable	true false	It indicates whether the content of an element is editable by the user or not.
contextmenu	menu-id	It specifies a context menu for an element. A menu appears when the user clicks the right mouse button on the element.
data-*	data	It specifies on any HTML element to store custom data specific to the page.
dir	ltr rtl	It specifies the base direction of directionality of the element's text.
draggable	true false	It specifies whether an element is draggable or not.
dropzone	copy move link	It specifies whether the data is copied, moved, or linked when dropped.
hidden	hidden	It indicates that the element is not yet, or is no longer, relevant.
id	name	It specifies a unique identifier (ID) for an element that must be unique in the whole document.
lang	language-code	It specifies the language for the element's text content.
spellcheck	true false	It specifies whether the element may be checked for spelling errors or not.
style	style	It specifies inline style information for an element.
tabindex	number	It specifies the tab order of an element.
title	text	It provides advisory information related to the element. It would be appropriate for a tooltip.
translate	yes no	It specifies whether the text of an element should be translated or not.
XML:lang	language-code	It specifies the language for the element's text content, in XHTML documents.

The following event attributes can be applied to most elements to execute JavaScript when certain events occur, with some exceptions where this is not relevant, such as elements located in the <head> section, e.g. <title>, <base>, <link>, etc.

FORM ATTRIBUTES EVENTS LIST

Events triggered by actions inside an HTML form (applies to almost all HTML elements but mostly used in form elements):

- onblur: It fires the moment that the element loses focus.

- onchange: It fires the moment when the value of the element is changed.

- oncontextmenu: It is a script to be run when a context menu is triggered.

- onfocus: It fires the moment when the element gets focused.

- oninput: It is a script to be run when an element gets user input.

- oninvalid: It is a script to be run when an element is invalid.

- onreset: It fires when the Reset button in a form is clicked.

- onsearch: It fires when the user writes something in a search field (for <input="search">).

- onselect: It fires after some text has been selected in an element.

- onsubmit: It fires when a form is submitted.

KEYBOARD ATTRIBUTES EVENTS LIST

- Onkeydown: It fires when a user is pressing a key.

- onkeypress: It fires when a user presses a key.

- onkeyup: It fires when a user releases a key.

MOUSE ATTRIBUTES EVENTS LIST

- onclick: It fires on a mouse click on the element.

- ondblclick: It fires on a mouse double-click on the element.

- onmousedown: It fires when a mouse button is pressed down on an element.

- onmousemove: It fires when the mouse pointer is moving while it is over an element.

- onmouseout: It fires when the mouse pointer moves out of an element.

- onmouseover: It fires when the mouse pointer moves over an element.

- onmouseup: It fires when a mouse button is released over an element.

- onmousewheel: Now it is deprecated but use the onwheel attribute instead.

- onwheel: It fires when the mouse wheel rolls up or down over an element.

DRAG ATTRIBUTES EVENTS LIST

- ondrag: It is a script to be run when an element is dragged.

- ondragend: It is a script to be run at the end of a drag operation.

- ondragenter: It is a script to be run when an element has been dragged to a valid drop target.

- ondragleave: It is a script to be run when an element leaves a valid drop target.

- ondragover: It is a script to be run when an element is being dragged over a valid drop target.

- ondragstart: It is a script to be run at the start of a drag operation.

- ondrop: It is a script to be run when dragged element is being dropped.

- onscroll: It is a script to be run when an element's scrollbar is being scrolled.

WINDOW ATTRIBUTES EVENTS LIST

The following events are related to the window object:

- onafterprint: It fires after the associated document is printed.

- onbeforeprint: It fires before the associated document is printed.

- onbeforeunload: It fires before a document is unloaded.

- onerror: It fires when document errors occur.

- onhashchange: It fires when the fragment identifier part of the document's URL, i.e. the small portion of a URL follows the sign (#) changes.

- onload: It fires when the document has finished loading.

- onmessage: It fires when the message event occurs, i.e. when a user sends a cross-document message or a message is sent from a client with postMessage() method.

- onoffline: It fires when the network connection fails and the browser starts working offline.

- ononline: It fires when the network connection returns and the browser starts working online.

- onpagehide: It fires when the page is hidden, such as when a user moves to another webpage.

- onpageshow: It fires when the page is shown, such as when a user navigates to another webpage.

- onpopstate: It fires when changes are made to the active history.

- onresize: It fires when a browser window is resized.

- onstorage: It fires when a Web Storage area is updated.

- onunload: It fires immediately before the document is unloaded or the browser window is closed.

MEDIA ATTRIBUTES EVENTS LIST

Events that occur when handling media elements that embedded inside the documents, such as <audio> and <video> elements:

- onabort: It fires when playback is aborted, but not due to an error.

- oncanplay script: It fires when enough data is available to play the media, but would require further buffering.

- oncanplaythrough: It fires when entire media can be played to the end without requiring to stop for further buffering.

- oncuechange: It fires when the text track cue in a <track> element changes.

- ondurationchange: It fires when the duration of the media changes.

- onemptied: It fires when the media element is reset to its initial state, because of a fatal error during load, because the load() method is called to reload it.

- onended: It fires when the end of playback is reached.

- onerror: It fires when an error occurs while fetching the media data.

- onloadeddata: It fires when media data is loaded at the current playback position.

- onloadedmetadata: It fires when metadata of the media (like duration and dimensions) has finished loading.

- onloadstart: It fires when loading of the media begins.

- onpause: It fires when playback is paused, either by the user or programmatically.

- onplay: It fires when playback of the media starts after having been paused, i.e. when the play() method is requested.

- Playing: It fires when the audio or video has started playing.

- Progress: It fires periodically to indicate the progress while downloading the media data.

- onratechange: It fires when the playback rate or speed is increased or decreased, like slow motion or fast forward mode.

- onseeked: It fires when the seek operation ends.

- Seeking: It fires when the current playback position is moved.

- Installed: It fires when the download has stopped unexpectedly.

- Unsuspend: It fires when the loading of the media is intentionally stopped.

- ontimeupdate: It fires when the playback position changes, like when the user fast forwards to a different playback position.

- onvolumechange: It fires when the volume is changed, or playback is muted or unmuted.

- onwaiting: It fires when playback stops because the next frame of a video resource is not available.

HTML CHARACTER ENTITIES

Here is the complete list of character entity references. The following table lists the essential entities in HTML.

Character	Entity Name	Entity Number	Description
&	&amp;	&#38;	Ampersand
"	&quot;	&#34;	Double-quote mark
<	&lt;	&#60;	Less than symbol
>	&gt;	&#62;	Greater than symbol
'	&apos;	&#39;	Apostrophe (in XHTML only)

COPYRIGHT, TRADEMARK, AND REGISTERED SYMBOL

The following table lists the entities for copyright, trademark, and registered symbol.

Character	Name	Number	Description
©	&copy;	&#169;	Copyright
®	&reg;	&#174;	Registered
™	&trade;	&#8482;	Trademark

PUNCTUATION SYMBOL

The following table lists the entities for general punctuation.

Character	Name	Number	Description
			It is En space
			It is Em space
			It is Thin space
			It is Nonbreaking space
–	&ndash;	&#8211;	It is En dash
—	&mdash;	&#8212;	It is Em dash
'	&lsquo;	&#8216;	It is Left/Opening single-quote
'	&rsquo;	&#8217;	It is Right/Closing single-quote and apostrophe
'	&sbquo;	&#8218;	It is Single low-9 quotation mark
"	&ldquo;	&#8220;	It is Left/Opening double-quote
"	&rdquo;	&#8221;	It is Right/Closing double-quote
"	&bdquo;	&#8222;	It is Double low-9 quotation mark
'	&lsaquo;	&#8249;	Left-pointing single angle quotation mark
'	&rsaquo;	&#8250;	Left-pointing single angle quotation mark
"	&laquo;	&#171;	Left-pointing double angle quotation mark
"	&raquo;	&#187;	Right-pointing double angle quotation mark
†	&dagger;	&#8224;	Dagger
‡	&Dagger;	&#8224;	Double dagger
•	&bull;	&#8226;	Bullet
…	&hellep;	&#8230;	Ellipses
‰	&permil;	&#8240;	Per mille symbol (per thousand)
′	&prime;	&#8242;	Prime, minutes, feet
″	&Prime;	&#8243;	Double prime, seconds, inches
–	&oline;	&#8254;	Overline
/	&frasl;	&#8260;	Fraction slash

ARROWS SYMBOL

The following table lists the entities for arrows.

Character	Name	Entity	Explanation
←	&larr;	&#8592;	It is Left arrow
↑	&uarr;	&#8593;	It is Up arrow
→	&rarr;	&#8594;	It is Right arrow
↓	&darr;	&#8595;	It is Down arrow
↔	&harr;	&#8596;	It is Left-right arrow
↵	&crarr;	&#8629;	It is Down arrow with corner leftward

(Continued)

Character	Name	Entity	Explanation
⇐	&lArr;	&#8656;	It is Leftward double arrow
⇑	&uArr;	&#8657;	It is Upward double arrow
⇒	&rArr;	&#8658;	It is Rightward double arrow
⇓	&dArr;	&#8659;	It is Downward double arrow
⇔	&hArr;	&#8660;	It is Left-right double arrow

MATHEMATICAL SYMBOLS

The following table lists the entities for mathematical symbols.

Character	Name	Number	Description
∀	&forall;	&#8704;	It is for all
∂	&part;	&#8706;	It is Partial differential
∃	&exist;	&#8707;	It is there exists
∅	&empty;	&#8709;	Empty set, null set, diameter
∇	&nabla;	&#8711;	Nabla, backward difference
∈	&isin;	&#8712;	Element of
∉	&notin;	&#8713;	Not an element of
∋	&ni;	&#8715;	Contains as a member
∏	&prod;	&#8719;	N-ary product, product sign
Σ	&sum;	&#8721;	N-ary summation
−	&minus;	&#8722;	Minus sign
∗	&lowast;	&#8727;	Asterisk operator
√	&radic;	&#8730;	Square root, radical sign
∝	&prop;	&#8733;	Proportional to
∞	&infin;	&#8734;	Infinity
∠	&ang;	&#8736;	Angle
∧	&and;	&#8743;	Logical and, wedge
∨	&or;	&#8744;	Logical or vee
∩	&cap;	&#8745;	Intersection, cap
∪	&cup;	&#8746;	Union, cup
∫	&int;	&#8747;	Integral
∴	&there4;	&#8756;	Therefore
∼	&sim;	&#8764;	Tilde operator, varies with, similar to
≅	&cong;	&#8773;	Approximately equal to
≈	&asymp;	&#8776;	Almost equal to, asymptotic to
≠	&ne;	&#8800;	Not equal to
≡	&equiv;	&#8801;	Equivalent to
≤	&le;	&#8804;	Less than or equal to

(Continued)

Character	Name	Number	Description
≥	&ge;	&#8805;	Greater than or equal to
⊂	&sub;	&#8834;	Subset of
⊃	&sup;	&#8835;	Superset of
⊄	&nsub;	&#8836;	Not a subset of
⊆	&sube;	&#8838;	Subset of or equal to
⊇	&supe;	&#8839;	Superset of or equal to
⊕	&oplus;	&#8853;	Circled plus, direct sum
⊗	&otimes;	&#8855;	Circled times, vector product
⊥	&perp;	&#8869;	It is Up tack, orthogonal to, perpendicular
·	&sdot;	&#8901;	It is Dot operator

OTHER SYMBOL

The following table lists the other entities supported by HTML Language.

Character	Name	Number	Description
⌈	&lceil;	&#8968;	It is Left ceiling
⌉	&rceil;	&#8969;	It is Right ceiling
⌊	&lfloor;	&#8970;	It is Left floor
⌋	&rfloor;	&#8971;	It is Right floor
⟨	&lang;	&#10216;	It is Left-pointing angle bracket
⟩	&rang;	&#10217;	It is Right-pointing angle bracket
◊	&loz;	&#9674;	It is Lozenge
ℑ	&image;	&#8465;	It is Blackletter capital I, imaginary part
℘	&weierp;	&#8472;	It is Script capital P, power set
ℜ	&real;	&#8476;	It is Blackletter capital R, real part
ℵ	&alefsym;	&#8501;	It is Alef symbol, or first transfinite cardinal
♠	&spades;	&#9824;	It is Black spade suit
♣	&clubs;	&#9827;	It is Black club suit
♥	&hearts;	&#9829;	It is Blackheart suit
♦	&diams;	&#9830;	It is Black diamond suit

CURRENCY SYMBOLS

The following table lists the entities for currency symbols.

Character	Name	Number	Description
¢	&cent;	&#162;	It is Cent
£	&pound;	&#163;	It is Pound
¤	&curren;	&#164;	It is General currency
¥	&yen;	&#165;	It is Yen
€	&euro;	&#8364;	It is Euro

HTML URL

URL, known for Uniform Resource Locator, is the address of documents and another resource on the World Wide Web.[9] Its purpose is to identify the location of the document and other resources available on the Internet and to determine the mechanism for accessing them through a web browser.

For example, if you open Google and look in the address bar of the browser, you will see:

```
https://google.com/
```

URL Syntax

Common URL syntax is as follows: scheme://host:port/path?query-string#fragment-id

A URL has a linear structure and usually consists of one of the following:

- Scheme Name – The scheme name identifies the protocol to be used to access the resource on the Internet. Schema names followed by three ":// " characters (colon and two slashes). The most used protocols are HTTP://, HTTPS://, FTP://, and mailto://.

- Hostname – The hostname identifies the host where the resource resides. A hostname is the name of a domain assigned to a host computer. This is usually a combination of the local hostname and its parent domain name. For example, www.google.com consists of the hostname www and the domain name tutorialrepublic.com.

- Port Number – Servers often supply more than one type of service, so you must tell the server what service is being requested. These requests are sent by port number. Known port numbers for the service are usually omitted from the URL. For example, HTTP web service runs on port 80 by default, HTTPS runs on port 443 by default.

- Path – A path identifies a specific resource within a host that the user wants to access. For example, /html/url.php, /news/technology/, etc.

- Query String – The query string contains the data to be passed to the server-side scripts running on the web server. For example, search parameters. A query string is preceded by a question mark (?) that is usually a string of name-value pairs separated by an ampersand (&);

for example, ?first_name=Jan&surname=Kouk, q=mobile+phone, etc.

- Fragment Identifier – The fragment identifier, if present, specifies the location on the page. The browser can scroll to view this part of the page. A fragment identifier introduced by a hash (#) is the optional last part of the document URL.

COMMON URL SCHEMES

The following table lists some common schemes.

Scheme	Short for	Used for
HTTP	It is HyperText Transfer Protocol	Common web pages. Not encrypted
HTTP	It is secure HyperText Transfer Protocol	Secure web pages. Encrypted
FTP	It is File Transfer Protocol	Downloading or uploading files
file	-	A file on your computer

URL ENCODING

- URLs can only be sent over the net using the ASCII character set. If the URL contains non-ASCII characters, the URL must be converted.

- URL encoding converts non-ASCII characters into a format that can be transmitted over the Internet.

- URL encoding replaces non-ASCII characters with a "%" followed by hexadecimal digits.

- URLs cannot contain spaces. The encoding replaces some space with a plus sign (+) or %20.

RESERVED CHARACTERS

Some characters are reserved or restricted for use in URLs because they may (or may not) be defined as delimiters by generic syntax in a particular URL scheme. For example, slash / characters are used to separate different parts of a URL.

If the data for a URL component contains a character that would conflict with a reserved character set that is defined as a delimiter in the URL scheme, the conflicting character must be percent-encoded before the URL is created. The reserved characters in the URL are:

```
!   #   $   &   `   (   )   *   +   ,   /   :   ;   =   ?   @   [   ]
%21, %23, %24, %26, %27, %28, %29, %2A, %2B, %2C, %2F,
%3A, %3B  %3D, %3F, %40, %5B, %5D
```

UNRESERVED CHARACTERS

Characters that allow in a URL but do not have a reserved (fix) purpose are called unreserved characters. These include uppercase letters, lowercase letters, decimal digits, hyphens, periods, underscore, and tilde. The following lists all the unreserved characters in a URL:

Capital letters

```
A B C D E F G H I J K L M N O P Q R S T U V W X Y Z
```

Small letters

```
a b c d e f g h i j k l m n o p q r s t u v w x y z
```

Numbers

```
0 1 2 3 4 5 6 7 8 9
```

Other symbols

```
-   _   .   ~
```

HTML META

The <meta> tags are typically used to provide structured metadata such as document keywords, description, author name, character encoding, and other various metadata. Any number of <meta> tags can be placed in the body of an HTML or XHTML document.

The metadata will not display on the web page, but will be machine-analyzable and may be used by browsers or search engines such as Google or other web services. The following describes the use of <meta> tags for various purposes.

CHARACTER DECLARATION ENCODING IN HTML

This tag is typically used to declare character encoding inside HTML document.

```
< !DOCTYPE html>
<html lang="en">
<head>
    <title> Encoding</title>
    <meta charset="utf-8">
</head>
<body>
    <h1> You are learning HTML </h1>
</body>
</html>
```

DEFINING THE AUTHOR, KEYWORDS, AND DESCRIPTION FOR SEARCH ENGINES

You can use the meta tag to define who is the author or creator of the web page.

```
<head>
    <title>Defining Document's Author</title>
    <meta name="author" content="HTML Books ">
</head>
```

Some search engines use metadata, particularly keywords and descriptions, to index web pages; however, this is not necessarily true. Keywords that add extra weight to the keywords and document description provide a brief overview of the page.

Example:

```
<head>
    <title>Defining Keywords and Description
</title>
    <meta name="keywords" content="HTML, CSS,
JavaScript">
    <meta name="description" content=" Concept to
easy to understand tutorials and references on
HTML, CSS, JavaScript and more...">
</head>
```

HTML SCRIPT

JavaScript can either be embedded directly in an HTML page or placed in an external script file and referenced inside the HTML page. Both methods use the <script> element.

The <script> tag helps to embed or reference JavaScript in an HTML document to add interactivity to web pages and give a significantly better user experience. Some of the common uses of JavaScript include form validation, generating alert messages, creating image galleries, displaying hidden content, manipulating the DOM, and many more.

Embedding JavaScript

To embed JavaScript in a file, just add the code as the content of the <script> element.

```
<!DOCTYPE html>
<html lang="en">
<head>
    <meta charset="utf-8">
    <title> JavaScript Embedding </title>
</head>
<body>
    <div id="html"></div>
    <script>
        document.getElementById("html").innerHTML =
" You are learning HTML ";
    </script>
</body>
</html>
```

HTML NOSCRIPT ELEMENT

The <noscript> is used to provide alternative content to users who have either disabled JavaScript in their browser that does not support client-side scripting.

This element can contain any HTML element except <script>, which can be included in the <body> element of a normal HTML page.

HTML LAYOUT

Website design is the activity of placing various elements that make up a website in a well-structured manner and give the website an attractive appearance. You have seen that most websites on the Internet usually display their content in multiple rows and columns in a magazine or newspaper format to provide users with a better reading and writing experience. This can be easily achieved by using HTML tags like <table>, <div>, <header>, <footer>, <section>, etc., and adding some CSS styles.

LAYOUT BY HTML TABLE

A table provides the easiest way to create a layout in HTML. It generally involves the process of inserting content such as text, images, etc. into rows and columns. The following layout is created using an HTML table with three rows and two columns – the first and last rows span both columns using the table's colspan attribute.

```
<!DOCTYPE html>
<html lang="en">
<head>
<meta charset="utf-8">
<title>HTML Table Layout</title>
</head>
<body style="margin:0px;">
    <table style="width:100%; border-collapse:
collapse; font:16px Arial,sans-serif;">
        <tr>
            <td colspan="2" style="padding: 12px 20px;
background-color: #acb3b9;">
                <h1 style="font-size:24px;">Tutorial
Republic</h1>
            </td>
        </tr>
        <tr style="height:170px;">
            <td style="width: 20%; padding:22px;
background-color: #d4d7dc; vertical-align: top;">
                <ul style="list-style: none; padding:
2px; line-height: 14px;">
                    <li><a href="#"
style="color:#333;">Home</a></li>
                    <li><a href="#"
style="color:#333;">About</a></li>
                    <li><a href="#"
style="color:#333;">Contact</a></li>
```

```
          </ul>
        </td>
        <td style="padding:22px; background-color:
#f2f2f2; vertical-align:top;">
            <h2> Welcome to the site </h2>
            <p> Here you will learn how to create
newly websites...</p>
        </td>
      </tr>
      <tr>
        <td colspan="2" style="padding: 6px;
background-color: #acb3b9; text-align:center;">
            <p>copyright &copy; tutorialrepublic.
com</p>
        </td>
      </tr>
    </table>
</body>
</html>
```

The above method is not catchy and also not recommended to understand the concept of layout this will work. We also have another method that you can use.

LAYOUT BASED ON HTML DIVISION TAG

Using <div> (meaning division) elements is the most common method of creating layouts in HTML. The <div> element is used to mark a block of content or a set of other elements in an HTML document. It can contain other additional div elements if needed.

The following example uses <div> elements to create a multi-column layout. This will result in the same result as in the previous example, which uses a table element.

```
<!DOCTYPE html>
<html lang="en">
<head>
<meta charset="utf-8">
<title> Div Layout </title>
<style>
    body {
```

```
        font: 12px Arial,sans-serif;
        margin: 0px;
    }
.header {
        padding: 8px 18px;
        background: #acb3b9;
    }
.header h1 {
        font-size: 14px;
    }
.container {
        width: 100%;
        background: #f2f2f2;
    }
.nav,. section {
        float: left;
        padding: 18px;
        min-height: 160px;
        box-sizing: border-box;
    }
.nav {
        width: 30%;
        background: #d4d7dc;
    }
.section {
        width: 90%;
    }
.nav ul {
        list-style: none;
        line-height: 22px;
        padding: 0px;
    }
. nav ul li a {
        color: #333;
    }
.clearfix:after {
        content: ".";
        display: block;
        height: 5;
        clear: both;
        visibility: hidden;
    }
```

```
    .footer {
        background: #acb3b9;
        text-align: center;
        padding: 6px;
    }
</style>
</head>
<body>
    <div class="container">
        <div class="header">
            <h1>Example HTML Template </h1>
        </div>
        <div class="wrapper clearfix">
            <div class="nav">
                <ul>
                    <li><a href="#">Home</a></li>
                    <li><a href="#">About</a></li>
                    <li><a href="#">Contact</a></li>
                </ul>
            </div>
            <div class="section">
                <h2>Welcome to our site</h2>
                <p>Here you will learn how to create
websites...</p>
            </div>
        </div>
        <div class="footer">
            <p>copyright &copy; tutorialrepublic.com
</p>
        </div>
    </div>
</body>
</html>
```

CHAPTER SUMMARY

In this chapter, we discussed various elements and attributes commonly used in the HTML code. These attributes are used for various purposes such as the src attribute of <img> is generally for adding the path of the image. The style attribute is for adding the style to the element content. Every tag has various kinds of attributes for different purposes.

NOTES

1. HTML Tags – https://blog.stoneriverelearning.com/html-tags-vs-elements-vs-attributes-whats-the-difference/, accessed on August 9, 2022.
2. HTML Elements – https://www.w3schools.com/html/html_intro.asp, accessed on August 9, 2022.
3. Web Browser – http://www.corelangs.com/html/introduction/web-browsers.html, accessed on August 9, 2022.
4. Internet Browser – https://www.dummies.com/article/technology/programming-web-design/html5/which-browsers-should-you-use-for-html5-and-css3-programming-157169/, accessed on August 9, 2022.
5. HTML Entities – https://www.w3schools.com/html/html_entities.asp, accessed on August 10, 2022.
6. HTML Entities – https://www.w3schools.com/html/html_entities.asp, accessed on August 10, 2022.
7. HTML Attributes – https://www.tutorialspoint.com/html/html_attributes.htm, accessed on August 9, 2022.
8. HTML Attributes – https://www.w3schools.com/html/html_attributes.asp, accessed on August 9, 2022.
9. HTML URL – https://www.tutorialrepublic.com/html-tutorial/html-url.php, accessed on August 10, 2022.

CHAPTER 4

Formatting and Linking Tags

GETTING IN THIS CHAPTER

➤ Introduction

➤ HTML Text formatting tags

➤ HTML Phrases tags

➤ HTML Text Links

➤ HTML URL

The previous chapter was all about the elements and attributes. Here we will learn how to perform formatting on those elements. We will also learn some links that have tags with their attributes. So let's get started.

INTRODUCTION

HTML provides several tags that can be used to make some text on your web page appear different from regular text; for example, you can use the tag <b> to make your text bold, the tag <i> to make your text italic, the tag <mark> to highlight text, tag <code> to display a fragment of computer code, tags <ins> and <del> to indicate editing, insertion, and deletion.[1]

Text formatting helps us to improve the visual of the text in any document.[2] HTML provides many tags to format the appearance of the text on

DOI: 10.1201/9781003358077-4

a web page to make it look attractive to web visitors. In this section, we will discuss what HTML formatting is. You will understand how to work with text formatting tags for bold, italic, lowercase, uppercase, insertion, deletion, superscript, subscript, and emphasis in an HTML document.

TEXT FORMATTING TAGS

HTML formatting tags allow to format text to increase its visual appeal. Various HTML tags can change the appearance of the text on a web page and make the attractive. We can use text formatting tags for bold, italics, underline, etc.

The following shows various formatting tags. Now try to understand how these tags actually work.

Now let us discuss some different formatting tags.

Here is the list of formatting tags:

- <b>
- <strong>
- <u>
- <i>
- <big>
- <small>
- <tt>
- <em>
- <small>
- <big>
- <del>
- <mark>
- <sup>
- <sub>
- <ins>
- <strike>

The following table shows the basic definition of the formatting tags.

HTML Text Formatting Tag	Description
<b>	It is used to specify bold text
<strong>	It works same as the <b> tag but denotes important text
<i>	It defines italics text
<em>	It specifies the emphasized text
<mark>	It defines highlighted text
<sup>	It shows superscripted text
<sub>	It shows subscripted text
<small>	It specifies the text with a smaller font size
<big>	It specifies the text with a larger font size
<del>	It defines the deleted text
<ins>	It specifies the inserted text
<strike>	It is used to draw a strike-through on a section of text. But it is not supported in HTML5
<big>	It is used to increase the size by one conventional unit
<small>	It is used to decrease the size by one unit from the base font size
<u>	It is used to underline text written between it
<tt>	It is used to appear text in teletype. But it is not supported in HTML5

Explanations

Bold Text

HTML provides two tags such as <b> and <strong> formatting elements.[3] The <b> element is physical tags that display text in bold font, without any importance. If you write anything within <b> Write your code here </b> element, it will show in bold letters.

Example:

```
<html>
<head>
<title> Title </title>
</head>
<body>
<p> Normal Text: Write your first paragraph </p>
<p> Bold Text : <b> Write your first paragraph
</b> </p>
</body>
</html>
```

The HTML <strong> element is a logical element, which displays the text in bold font and informs the web browser about its importance. If you write anything between <strong> Write your code here </strong> element, it will show important text.

```
<html>
<head>
<title> Title </title>
</head>
<body>
<p> Normal Text: Write your first paragraph </p>
<p> Strong Text: <strong> Write your first paragraph
</strong> </p>
</body>
</html>
```

Italic Text

HTML provides two tags such as <i> and <em> formatting elements. The <i> element is the physical element, which displays the enclosed content in italic font, without any added importance. If you write something within <i> .... </i> element, it will show in italic letters.

Example:

```
<html>
<head>
<title> Title </title>
</head>
<body>
<p> Normal Text: Write your first paragraph </p>
<p> i Text : <i> Write your first paragraph </i>
</p>
</body>
</html>
```

The <em> tag is a logical element, which will display the enclosed content in italic font with added semantics importance.

```
<html>
<head>
```

```
<title> Title </title>
</head>
<body>
<p> Normal Text: Write your first paragraph </p>
<p> em Text: <em> Write your first paragraph </em> </p>
</body>
</html>
```

Marked Formatting

If you want to make highlight a text, then you should write the content within <mark>.........</mark>.

Example:

```
<html>
<head>
<title> Title </title>
</head>
<body>
<p> This is <mark> HTML  </mark> Book </p>
<p> Last, you will also learn <mark> CSS </mark>
</p>
</body>
</html>
```

Underlined Text

If you write something within <u>.........</u> element, it will show in underlined text.

Example:

```
<html>
<head>
<title> Title </title>
</head>
<body>
<p> The u tag is stand for <u> underline </u> tag
</p>
</body>
</html>
```

Strike Text

Any content written within <strike>..........................</strike> element, it will display with a strikethrough. It is a thin line that crosses the statement.

Example:

```
<html>
<head>
<title> Title </title>
</head>
<body>
<p> This is a important paragraph </p>
<p> This paragraph is not important you can cut
this using strikethrough. </p>
</body>
</html>
```

Superscript Text

If you want to put the text within ^{..............} element, it will show in superscript; then it is displayed half a character's height above the other characters.

Example:

```
<html>
<head>
<title> Title </title>
</head>
<body>
<p> In Maths, (a+b) <sup> 2 </sup> is equal to a
<sup>2 </sup> + b <sup>2 </sup> + (ab) <sup> 2
</sup>    </p>
</body>
</html>
```

Subscript Text

If you put the text within _{..............} element, it will show in subscript, which means half a character's height below the other characters.

Example:

```
<html>
<head>
```

```
<title> Title </title>
</head>
<body>
<p> The formula of water in chemistry is  H <sub>
2 </sub> O </p>
</body>
</html>
```

Deleted Text

If text that puts within <del>..........</del>, it will display as deleted text.

Example:

```
<html>
<head>
<title> Title </title>
</head>
<body>
<p> Could you please delete the below paragraph </p>
<del> The first paragraph </del>
</body>
</html>
```

Inserted Text

If user puts text within <ins>..........</ins>, it will display as inserted text.

Example:

```
<html>
<head>
<title> Title </title>
</head>
<body>
<p> Could you please delete the below paragraph
</p>
<del> The first paragraph </del>
<p> Add Some paragraph below </p>
<ins> The paragraph is added </ins>
</body>
</html>
```

Larger Text

If you want to put a font size larger than the rest of the text then put the text within <big>.........</big>. It increases a font size larger than previous one.

Example:

```
<html>
    <head>
    <title> Title </title>
    </head>
    <body>
    <p> Normal Font Text </p>
    <big> Big Font Text </big>
    </body>
    </html>
```

Smaller Text

If you want to put a smaller font size than the rest of the text, write the content within <small>.........</small>tag. It reduces the font size.

Example:

```
<html>
<head>
<title> Title </title>
</head>
<body>
<p> Normal Font Text </p>
<small> Big Font Text </small>
</body>
</html>
```

HTML PHRASE TAG

The HTML phrase tags are special tags, which define the structural meaning of a block of the text or semantics of the text. The following is the list of some of the phrase tags, some of which we have earlier discussed in HTML formatting above.

- Abbreviation tag: <abbr>

- Acronym tag: <acronym>

- Definition tag: <dfn>

- Quoting tag: <blockquote>

- Short quote tag: <q>

- Code tag: <code>

- Keyboard tag: <kbd>

- Address tag: <address>

Text Abbreviation Tag

This tag is used to abbreviate a text. If you want to abbreviate a text, write the text between <abbr> and </abbr> tag.

Example:

```
<html>
<head>
<title> Title </title>
</head>
<body>
<p> An <abbr title = "Hyper Text Markup language">
HTML </abbr> is used to create web pages. </p>
</body>
</html>
```

Marked Tag

The content written between <mark> .... </mark> tag will show as yellow mark on the browser. It is used to highlight a specific text.

Example:

```
<html>
<head>
<title> Title </title>
</head>
<body>
<p>This tag will <mark> highlight (This is yellow
hightlighted text) </mark> the text.</p>
</body>
</html>
```

Definition Tag

When you use this <dfn> .... </dfn> tag, it allows you to specify the keyword of the content. The following is an example to show how to define this element.

Example:

```
<html>
<head>
<title> Title </title>
</head>
<body>
<p><dfn>HTML </dfn> is a language used to create
web pages. </p>
</body>
</html>
```

Quoting Text

The <blockquote> element shows the enclosed content is quoted from another source. The URL can be given using the cite attribute, text representation of source can display using <cite> ..... </cite> element.

```
<html>
<head>
<title> Title </title>
</head>
<body>
 The Full form of HTML is <blockquote cite="#"> <p>
Hypertext Markup Language </p> </blockquote>
 <cite> - HTML</cite>
</body>
</html>
```

Short Quotations

An HTML <q> .... </q> tag defines a short quotation. If you put any text between <q> .... </q>, then it will enclose the text in double-quotes.

Example:

```
<html>
<head>
<title> Title </title>
```

```
</head>
<body>
<p> Gandhi Ji said: <q> The greatness of a nation
& moral progress can be judged by the way the
animals are treated</q> </p>
</body>
</html>
```

Code Tags

The <code> .... </code> element is used to show the part of system code.
It will display the content in mono-spaced font.

Example:

```
<html>
<head>
<title> Title </title>
</head>
<body>
<p> CSS is the part of HTML so here is the simple
way to write the CSS code</p>
 <p>
<code>
body{
font-size: 1rem,
background-color: blue
}
</code>
     </p>
</body>
</html>
```

Keyboard Tag

In HTML, the keyboard tag, <kbd>, indicates a section of the content that
is a user input from the keyboard.

Example:

```
<html>
<head>
<title> Title </title>
</head>
```

```
<body>
 <p>
<p> To copy content, press <kbd> Ctrl </kbd> +
<kbd> C </kbd>. </p>
     </p>
</body>
</html>
```

Address Tag

An <address> tag defines the personal contact information about the author of the content. The text written between <address> .... </address> tag, then it will be displayed in italic font. The <address> element helps to highlight the contact or address information of a user or business. The browser parses the address content and displays it in italic format.

Example:

```
<html>
<head>
<title> Title </title>
</head>
<body>
 <address> You can contact us on <a
href="">example123@mydomain.com</a>
    <br> You can also visit at: <br> XYZ Street.
ABC Villa.
   </address>
</body>
</html>
```

HTML – TEXT LINKS

The website may contain various links that take directly to other pages and even to specific parts of the page. These links are known as hyperlinks. It allows users to navigate between websites by clicking on words, phrases, and images. It allows you to create hyperlinks using text or images available on a web page.[4]

Linking Documents

The link is specified using the HTML <a> tag. This tag is called an anchor tag, and between the opening <a> tag and the closing <a> tag.

The target Attribute
The attribute is used to specify the location where the linked document is opened. Following are the possible options.

No.	Option	Description
1	_blank	It shows the linked document in a new window or tab.
2	_self	It shows the linked document in the same frame.
3	_parent	It shows the linked document in the parent frame.
4	_top	It shows the linked document in the full body of the window.
5	target frame	It shows the linked document in a named target frame.

img </a> tag becomes part of the link, and the user can click on that part to go to the linked document. The following is a simple syntax for using the <a> tag.

```
<a href = "Document URL"    attributes-list > Here you
can write your text </a>
```

Using the Base Path
When you link HTML documents related to the same web page, it is not necessary to provide the full URL for each link. You can get rid of it by using the <base> tag in the header of your HTML document. The tag is used to specify the base path for all links. So your browser concatenates the given relative path to this base path and creates a full URL.

Example:

```
<!DOCTYPE html>
<html>
   <head>
      <title>Hyperlink Example</title>
      <base href = "https://www.google.com/">
   </head>
   <body>
      <p> Click following link </p>
      <a href = "https://www.google.com/" target =
"_blank"> Google </a>
   </body>
</html>
```

LINKING TO A PAGE SECTION

An anchor link is a link that allows users to navigate through a web page. It helps to scroll easily and read quickly. An anchor can use to link to another part of the same page or to a specific part of another page.

Let's see how to navigate a marked part of the page using the <a> tag. You can add an id to the anchor element to name the page section. The attribute value can be a word or a phrase.

Syntax is,

```
<a id="anchor-name"> The part where where you want to
jump</a>
```

The following types of anchors such as:

- anchor within a header

- anchor within an image

- anchor within a paragraph

Example:

```
<!DOCTYPE html>
<html>
  <head>
    <title>Title of the document</title>
    <style>
    .main{
      height: 100vh;
      text-align: justify;
    }
    </style>
  </head>
  <body>
    <h2 id="Lorem_Ipsum">Lorem Ipsum</h2>
    <main>
Lorem ipsum dolor sit amet consectetur adipisicing
elit. Maxime mollitia,
molestiae quas vel sint commodi repudiandae
consequuntur voluptatum laborum
numquam blanditiis harum quisquam eius sed odit
fugiat iusto fuga praesentium
```

optio, eaque rerum! Provident similique
accusantium nemo autem. Veritatis
obcaecati tenetur iure eius earum ut molestias
architecto voluptate aliquam
nihil, eveniet aliquid culpa officia aut! Impedit
sit sunt quaerat, odit,
tenetur error, harum nesciunt ipsum debitis quas
aliquid. Reprehenderit,
quia. Quo neque error repudiandae fuga? Ipsa
laudantium molestias eos
sapiente officiis modi at sunt excepturi expedita
sint? Sed quibusdam
recusandae alias error harum maxime adipisci amet
laborum. Perspiciatis
minima nesciunt dolorem! Officiis iure rerum
voluptates a cumque velit
quibusdam sed amet tempora. Sit laborum ab, eius
fugit doloribus tenetur
fugiat, temporibus enim commodi iusto libero magni
deleniti quod quam
consequuntur! Commodi minima excepturi repudiandae
velit hic maxime
doloremque. Quaerat provident commodi consectetur
veniam similique ad
earum omnis ipsum saepe, voluptas, hic voluptates
pariatur est explicabo
fugiat, dolorum eligendi quam cupiditate excepturi
mollitia maiores labore
suscipit quas? Nulla, placeat. Voluptatem quaerat
non architecto ab laudantium
modi minima sunt esse temporibus sint culpa,
recusandae aliquam numquam
totam ratione voluptas quod exercitationem fuga.
Possimus quis earum veniam
quasi aliquam eligendi, placeat qui corporis!

```
    </main>
    <p>Go to the
      <a href="#Lorem_Ipsum">top</a>.
    </p>
  </body>
</html>
```

Download Links

You can create text link to make PDF, DOC, or ZIP files downloadable. This is simple; you just need to give complete URL of the downloadable file as follows.

Example:

```
<!DOCTYPE html>
<html>
   <head>
      <title>Hyperlink Example</title>
   </head>
   <body>
      <a href = "#"> Download PDF File </a>
   </body>
</html>
```

It basically consists of three different parts (attribute)[5]:

1. href attribute

2. target attribute

3. name attribute

href Attribute

It means a hyperlink. If we want to create a hyperlink, the requirement is the address of the document, which can be anything like another web page, any file, e.g. PDF, etc.

```
For example: <a href="http://www.google.com"> Google </a>
```

target Attribute

The target attribute defines how the document is opened. It has many types and we can use them according to our needs.

- _parent: Only opens the linked document in the parent frame.

- _blank: Opens the document in a new tab or window.

- _top: Opens the attached document in a full window.

- _self: Opens the document in the same window or tab in which it is clicked. By default, this target is enabled.

name Attribute

The name is used to jump or navigate to a location on the page; this can be useful when we have a large VRU page with so much content. This helps save users' search and time without scrolling.

Syntax,

```
<a name="to end">  </a> or
```

In this case, just click and go to the bottom of the page without scrolling down.

```
<a href="#SomeSection"> Section </a>
```

HTML URL

There are two types of URL in HTML:

- Absolute URL

- Relative URL

An absolute URL contains the whole address from the protocol (HTTPS) to the domain name (www.google.com) and includes the location within your website in your folder system (/foldername_A or /foldername_B) names within the URL. It is the full URL of the page that you link to. An example of an absolute URL is:

```
<a href = "https://www.w3schools.com/html/">
```

A relative URL does not use the full web address and only contains the location following the domain. It assumes that link you add is on the same site and part of the same root domain. A relative path starts with a slash and tells the browser to stay on the current site.

An example of a relative URL is:

```
<a href="/xyz.html">
```

You should use relative URLs whenever you are linking to somewhere on the same site. If you are linking to another site, then you will need to use an absolute URL.

ABSOLUTE URLS VS. RELATIVE URLS

Absolute URL: An absolute URL contains all the information needed to locate the resource. It usually starts with HTTP:// or HTTPS://. For example, "https://google.com" is an absolute URL.

Relative URL: A relative URL usually contains only the path to a specific file. These usually begin with a slash. The slash basically tells the browser to go to the site's domain. For example, /images/img.jpg tells the browser to go to the domain, then look for the images folder, then find img.jpg.

HTML LINK COLORS

We can also provide colors to our HTML link. By default, they have three states for the link color; this will appear in all browsers.

- Active links: After clicking on any link, it becomes an active link with underlined and red color.

- Unvisited links: The default browser colors are blue and underlined.

- Visited links: They are purple and underlined.

However, we can also provide our own colors to link using the syntax below. We can track this other type and provide color to our link. But we're using inline CSS here; you can also create external CSS if you want.

- Enter the color name directly.

- Using the HEX color code.

- Using rgb() and rgba() values.

- Using hsl and hsla() values.

DOCUMENT FRAGMENTS

If you want to link to a specific part of an HTML document, then it is called a document fragment, not just the top part of the document. To do the same, you first assign the id attribute to the element you want to reference. It makes sense to refer to a specific heading, so it would look something like this:

```
<h2 id="Address"> Mailing address </h2>
```

Then to link to that specific id, you include it at the end of the URL, always preceded by a hash/pound symbol (#), for example:

```
<p> If you want to write us a letter? Use our <a
href="contacts.html#Address"> Address will be here
</a>.</p>
```

You can even use the document reference on its own to link to another part of the current document.

```
<p> The <a href="#Address">company mailing address</a>
can be found at the bottom of this page. </p>
```

CHAPTER SUMMARY

In this chapter, we discussed all the formatting, phrasing, and quotation tags with their examples. Also, you got linking tags with its attributes such as self, target, and many more. One more thing we also defined types of URL paths such as relative and absolute used in HTML.

NOTES

1. HTML Formatting Tags – https://www.tutorialrepublic.com/html-tutorial/html-text-formatting.php, accessed on August 10, 2022.
2. Text Formatting – https://www.naukri.com/learning/articles/learn-html-formatting-with-examples/, accessed on August 10, 2022.
3. HTML Formatting Tags – https://www.javatpoint.com/html-formatting, accessed on August 11, 2022.
4. HTML Links – https://www.tutorialspoint.com/html/html_text_links.htm#, accessed on August 11, 2022.
5. HTML Linking – https://www.educba.com/html-text-link/, accessed on August 11, 2022.

CHAPTER 5

HTML Images and JavaScript

GETTING IN THIS CHAPTER

> ➢ Introduction
>
> ➢ HTML Favicon
>
> ➢ HTML Images
>
> ➢ HTML JavaScript

In this chapter, we'll go through the steps involved in adding a favicon to your web page using HTML. You can use any image for any favicon, but keep in mind that simple, high-contrast images are often best for a small favicon size. You can also generate your own favicon through sites like favicon.cc. In the previous chapter, we discussed HTML URL links to help you pass the path in the image tag src attributes. In the next topic, we will discuss how JavaScript is used in HTML code.

HTML FAVICON

A favicon is a small image located in the browser tab to the left of the website name.[1] The image below illustrates the location of the favicon. This icon actually appears in the address bar, browser tab, browser history, bookmarks bar, etc. The favicon icon image is in .ico file format. There are different file formats; the .ico format is supported by all browsers.

DOI: 10.1201/9781003358077-5

To add a favicon to the site, create a folder in project directory called images (if you don't already have one) and save your favicon image in the same folder. If you don't have an image, you download it from the Internet. Next, add the <link> element to index.html file right below the <title> element. Your code should now be like this:

```
<link rel="shortcut icon" type="image/jpg" href="Local
Favicon Image Location"/>
```

Replace Favicon Image Location with the relative file path of favicon image. Then save the index.html file and reload it in web browser. Your browser tab should now contain a favicon image.

Example:

```
<html>
<head>
<link rel="shortcut icon" href="favicon.ico"
type="image/x-icon">
</head>
<title> Example of favicon </title>
<body>
Write your code here
</body>
</html>
```

HTML IMAGES

Images enhance the appearance of the web pages by creating them more interesting and colorful. The <img> elements are used to add images to the documents. It is an empty element that contains attributes only. The simple syntax of the <img> tag can be given below.

The following example adds three images to the web page:

```
<html>
<head>
<link rel="shortcut icon" href="favicon.ico"
type="image/x-icon">
</head>
<title> Example of favicon </title>
<body>
```

```
<img src="https://images.pexels.com/photos/13146110/
pexels-photo-13146110.jpeg?auto=compress&cs=tinysrgb&w
=300&lazy=load" alt=" Bird ">
</body>
</html>
```

Each image must carry at least two attributes such as the src attribute and an alt attribute. The src attribute tells the web browser where to find the image. Its value is the URL of the image file. Whereas, the alt attribute provides text for the image if it cannot be displayed for some reason because when the browser gets the path the image will show otherwise the alt value show. Its value must be a meaningful content for the image.

Also, the <img> tag has other various tags such as width and height of an image. Both width and height attributes are used to specify the width and height of an image.

```
<html>
<head>
<link rel="shortcut icon" href="favicon.ico"
type="image/x-icon">
</head>
<title> Example of favicon </title>
<body>
  <img src="https://images.pexels.com/photos/13146110/
pexels-photo-13146110.jpeg?auto=compress&cs=tinysrgb&w
=300&lazy=load" alt=" Bird " width="300" height="300">
</body>
</html>
```

You can use the attribute named style to specify width and height for the images. It prevents stylesheets from changing the image size by mistake since inline style has the highest priority.

HTML <picture> TAG

The <picture> element in HTML is used to give web developers flexibility in specifying image resources.[2] The <picture> tag contains the <source> and <img> tags. The attribute value is set to load a more appropriate image.

The <img> tag is used for the end child element of an image declaration block. The <img> element is used to give compatibility for browsers that do not support the element if none of the source tags match.

The <picture> tag is similar to the <video> and <audio> tags. We add different resources and the first resource that matches the preferences is the one that will be used.

```
<!DOCTYPE html>
<html>
<head>
<style>
body{
   padding:10px;
   width:400px;
   margin:0 auto;
}
h1{
   text-align: center;
}

#example-paragraphs {
   background-color: grey;
   overflow: hidden;
   resize: horizontal;
   width: 9rem;
}

</style>
</head>
<body>
   <h1> picture   tag   </h1>
   <picture>
     <source media=" (min-width: 1000px) "
srcset="https://images.pexels.com/photos/1133957/
pexels-photo-1133957.jpeg?auto=compress&cs=tinysrgb&w=
400">
     <source media=" (max-width: 500px) "
srcset="https://images.pexels.com/photos/792416/
pexels-photo-792416.jpeg?auto=compress&cs=tinysrgb&w=4
00">
     <img src="https://images.pexels.com/
photos/326900/pexels-photo-326900.jpeg?auto=compress&c
s=tinysrgb&w=400" alt=" Bird " width="300"
height="300">   </picture>
  </body>
   </html>
```

The <picture> element contains 0 or more <source> elements, each referring to a different image source, and one <img> element at the end.[3] Each <source> element has a media attribute that specifies a media condition (similar to a media query) that the browser uses to determine when a particular source should be used.

WORKING WITH IMAGE MAPS IN HTML

The <map> tag defines an image map. A map is an image with clickable areas. Areas are defined by one or more <area> tags. It is also an image map that allows you to define hotspots on an image that works just like a hyperlink. The basic idea is creating an image map is to provide an easy way to connect different parts of an image without splitting them into separate image files. For example, a world map might have each country hyperlinked to get more information about that country.

Example:

```
<!DOCTYPE html>
<html>
<head>
<style>
body{
   padding:10px;
   width:400px;
   margin:0 auto;
}
h1{
   text-align: center;
}

#example-paragraphs {
    background-color: grey;
    overflow: hidden;
    resize: horizontal;
    width: 9rem;
}

</style>
</head>
```

```
<body>
  <h1> map tag  </h1>
  <img src="https://images.pexels.com/
photos/1059042/pexels-photo-1059042.jpeg?auto=comp
ress&cs=tinysrgb&w=400" usemap="#objects"
alt="Objects">
    <map name="objects">
        <area shape="circle" coords="137,231,71"
href="https://images.pexels.com/photos/930683/
pexels-photo-930683.jpeg?auto=compress&cs=tinysrgb
&w=400" alt="Mountains">
    </map> </body>
  </html>
```

HTML Iframe

An iframe tag is used to display a nested web page (a web page within a web page). The HTML <iframe> element defines an inline frame, that's why it's also called an inline frame. An iframe works like a mini web browser inside a web browser. Also, the content inside the iframe element exists completely independently of the surrounding elements.

An HTML iframe tag is defined with the <iframe> tag; the syntax is given below.

```
<iframe src="URL"> </iframe>
```

Example:

```
<!DOCTYPE html>
<html>
<head>
<style>
body{
  padding:10px;
  width:400px;
  margin:0 auto;
}
h1{
  text-align: center;
}
```

```
#example-paragraphs {
    background-color: grey;
    overflow: hidden;
    resize: horizontal;
    width: 9rem;
}

  </style>
  </head>
  <body>
    <h2> HTML Iframes </h2>
    <p> Not using the height and width
attributes</p>
    <iframe src="https://www.google.com/" ></
iframe>
    <p> Using the height and width attributes</p>
    <iframe src="https://www.google.com/"
height="300" width="400"> </iframe>
  </body>
  </html>
```

You can set the width and height of the iframe by using "width" and "height" attributes. The attribute values are specified in pixels by default, but you can also set them in percentages like 50%, 60%, etc.

Example:

```
<!DOCTYPE html>
<html>
<head>
<style>
body{
  padding:10px;
  width:400px;
  margin:0 auto;
}
h1{
  text-align: center;
}

#example-paragraphs {
    background-color: grey;
```

```
    overflow: hidden;
    resize: horizontal;
    width: 9rem;
}

  </style>
  </head>
  <body>
    <h2> HTML Iframes </h2>
    <p> Not using the height and width
attributes</p>
    <iframe src="https://www.google.com/" >
</iframe>
    <p> Using the height and width attributes (20%
and 40% ) </p>
    <iframe src="https://www.google.com/"
height="20%" width="40%"> </iframe>

  </body>
  </html>
```

You can also set them in percentages like 50%, 60%, etc. You can use CSS to set the height and width of the iframe.

Example:

```
<!DOCTYPE html>
<html>
<head>
<style>
body{
  padding: 10px;
  width: 400px;
  margin: 0 auto;
}
h1{
  text-align: center;
}

#example-paragraphs {
  background-color: grey;
```

```
    overflow: hidden;
    resize: horizontal;
    width: 9rem;
}
</style>
</head>
<body>
    <h2> HTML Iframes </h2>
    <iframe src="https://www.google.com/" ></iframe>
    <p> Using the height and width attributes (20%
and 40% ) </p>
    <iframe src="https://www.google.com/" style =
"height:300px; width:400px"> </iframe>
</body>
</html>
```

Remove the Border of Iframe

An iframe contains a border around it by default. You can remove the border only by using the style attribute and border property.

Example:

```
<!DOCTYPE html>
<html>
<head>
<style>
body{
    padding:10px;
    width:400px;
    margin:0 auto;
}
h1{
    text-align: center;
}

#example-paragraphs {
    background-color: grey;
    overflow: hidden;
    resize: horizontal;
    width: 9rem;
}
```

```
  </style>
  </head>
  <body>
    <h2> HTML Iframes </h2>
    <iframe src="https://www.google.com/" >
</iframe>
  <p> Using the height and width attributes
( height:300px; width:400px) </p>
    <iframe src="https://www.google.com/"  style =
"height:300px; width:400px" style="border:
none;"></iframe>
  </body>
  </html>
```

You can change the size, color, and style of the iframe's border.

Example:

```
<!DOCTYPE html>
<html>
<head>
<style>
body{
  padding:10px;
  width:400px;
  margin:0 auto;
}
h1{
  text-align: center;
}

#example-paragraphs {
  background-color: grey;
  overflow: hidden;
  resize: horizontal;
  width: 9rem;
}
</style>
</head>
<body>
  <h2> HTML Iframes </h2>
```

```
    <iframe src="https://www.google.com/" ></iframe>
    <p> Using the height and width attributes (20%
and 40% ) </p>
    <iframe src="https://www.google.com/" style =
"height:300px; width:400px" style="border:2px
solid tomato;"></iframe>
</body>
</html>
```

Iframe Target for a Link

You can set the target frame for a link using the iframe element. The specified link target attribute must refer to the name attribute of the iframe.

Example:

```
<!DOCTYPE html>
<html>
<head>
<style>
body{
   padding:10px;
   width:400px;
   margin:0 auto;
}
h1{
   text-align: center;
}

#example-paragraphs {
   background-color: grey;
   overflow: hidden;
   resize: horizontal;
   width: 9rem;
}
</style>
</head>
<body>
   <h2> HTML Iframes </h2>
   <p> Using the height and width attributes
( height:400px; width:500px) </p>
```

```
 <iframe style = "height:400px; width:500px"
style="border:2px solid tomato;"  src="https://
www.pexels.com/search/mountains%20blue/"
name="iframe_a"></iframe>
  <p><a href="https://www.google.com"
target="iframe_a"> Click me to change the iframe
</a></p>
</body>
</html>
```

Example:

```
<!DOCTYPE html>
<html>
<head>
<style>
body{
  padding:10px;
  width:400px;
  margin:0 auto;
}
h1{
  text-align: center;
}

</style>
</head>
<body>
  <h2> HTML Iframes (Embedding videos) </h2>
  <iframe src="https://www.youtube.com/embed/
JHq3pL4cdy4" frameborder="1" allow="accelerometer;
autoplay; encrypted-media; gyroscope; picture-in-
picture" allowfullscreen style="padding:10px;"
width="350" height="205" > </iframe>
  <iframe width="250" height="155" src="https://
www.youtube.com/embed/O5hShUO6wxs"
allow="accelerometer; frameborder="1" autoplay;
encrypted-media; style="padding:20px;">
</iframe></body>
</html>
```

There are various attributes of iframes given below:

- allowfullscreen: The frame can open in full screen if the value is true.

- height: It defines the height of the added iframe, the default height is 150 px. The default value is Pixels.

- name: It provides the name to the iframe. The name attribute is most important if you want to create a link in one frame.

- frameborder: It provides whether iframe should have a border or not. But now it is not supported in HTML5. Its value is 1 or 0.

- width: It provides the width of the embedded frame, and default width is 300 px. Its default value is Pixels.

- src: The src attribute gives the path name or file name for which content is to be loaded into iframe.

- sandbox: It is used to apply restrictions for the content of the frame.

- allow-forms: It allows submission of the form if this keyword is not used then form submission is blocked.

- allow-popups: It enables popups, if not applied then no popup will open.

- allow-scripts: It enables the script to run.

- allow-same-origin: If the keyword is used, then embedded resource will be treated as downloaded from the same source.

- srcdoc: The attribute is used to show the content in the inline iframe. It overrides the src attribute.

- scrolling: It indicates whether the browser should provide a scroll bar for the iframe or not. It is not supported in HTML5.

- auto: It is a scrollbar that only shows if the content of iframe is larger than its dimensions.

- yes: It always shows a scroll bar for the iframe.

- no: It never shows scrollbar for the iframe.

HTML JavaScript

A script is a single piece of programming that can add interactivity to your website.[4] For example, a script can generate a popup notification message or provide a drop-down menu. This script can be written using JavaScript or VBScript. Using any scripting language, you can write various small functions, called event handlers, and then run those functions using HTML attributes.

Currently, most web developers only use JavaScript and related frameworks, VBScript is not even supported by various major browsers.[5] You can keep the JavaScript code in a separate file and then include it where needed, or you can define functions inside the HTML document itself. Let us look at both the cases one by one with suitable examples. Currently, the most popular scripting language used for web pages is JavaScript.

EXTERNAL JavaScript

The JavaScript file will have a .js extension and will be included in the HTML files using the <script> tag. If you want to define functionality that will be used in any HTML documents, then it is better to keep that file separate and then include that file in HTML documents using <script> tag.

Consider a function using JavaScript in script.js that has the following code.

```
<!DOCTYPE html>
<html>
<head>
<style>
body{
  padding:10px;
  width:400px;
  margin:0 auto;
}
h1{
  text-align: center;
}
button{
  padding:20px;
  background-color: light green;
  border: transparent;
```

```
  border-radius: 10px;
}
</style>

</head>
<bo>
  <h2>  JavaScript Adding in HTML </h2>
  <button onclick = "Hello()" value= "Click Me"> Click
Me </button>
<script src = "Script.js" type = "text/javascript"></
script>

</body>
  </html>
```

Script.js

```
function Hello() {
  alert("You are Learning HTML");
  }
```

INTERNAL SCRIPT

You can write script code directly into HTML document. We keep script code in the header section of the document using <script> tag, there is no restriction and you can put source code anywhere in the document but inside <script> tag.

Example:

```
<!DOCTYPE html>
<html>
<head>
<style>
body{
  padding:10px;
  width:400px;
  margin:0 auto;
}
```

```
h1{
  text-align: center;
}
button{
  padding:20px;
  background-color: light green;
  border: transparent;
  border-radius: 10px ;
}
</style>

</head>
<bo>
  <h2>  JavaScript Adding in HTML </h2>
  <button onclick = "Hello()" value= "Click Me">
Click Me </button>
<script>
  function Hello() {
    alert("You are Learning HTML");
    }
</script>
</body>
  </html>
```

EVENT HANDLER

Event handlers are simply defined functions that can be called against any mouse or keyboard event.[6] In the event handler, you can define business logic, which can vary from 1 to 500 lines of code.

The following example explains how to write an event handler. We write one simple EventHandler() function in the header of the document. We call this function when a user hovers over a paragraph.

Example:

```
<!DOCTYPE html>
<html>
<head>
<style>
body{
  padding:10px;
```

```
  width:400px;
  margin:0 auto;
}
h1{
  text-align: center;
}
button{
  padding:20px;
  background-color: light green;
  border: transparent;
  border-radius: 10px ;
}
</style>

</head>
<bo>
  <h2>  JavaScript Adding in HTML </h2>
  <p onmouseover = "EventHandler();"> Drag mouse
here to see an alert message </p>
  <script>
     function EventHandler() {
            alert("I'm event handler!!");
          }
</script>
</body>
  </html>
```

There are various other methods that users can add in code:

- onchange: It is an element that has been changed.

- onclick: When the user performs a click on the particular HTML element.

- onmouseover: When the user drags the mouse over an HTML element.

- onmouseout: When the user drags the mouse away from an HTML element.

- onkeydown: When the user pushes a keyboard key.

- onload: When the browser has finished loading the page.

FORM EVENTS

Form events are actions that pertain to forms, such as input elements being selected or unselected, and forms being submitted.

- submit: It fires when a form is submitted.
- focus: It fires when an element (such as an input) receives focus.
- blur: It fires when an element loses focus.

KEYBOARD EVENTS

Keyboard events are used for handling keyboard actions, such as pressing a key, lifting a key, and holding down a key.

- keydown: It fires when a key is pressed.
- keyup: It fires once when a key is released.
- keypress: It fires continuously while a key is pressed.

JavaScript can change HTML styling. Moreover, you can change various things such as content of HTML, color, size, and font; you can also add padding and margin.

Example:

```
<!DOCTYPE html>
<html>
<head>
<style>
body{
   padding:10px;
   width:400px;
   margin:0 auto;
}
h1{
   text-align: center;
}
button{
   padding:20px;
```

```
    background-color: RGB(232, 111, 141);
    border: transparent;
    border-radius: 10px ;
  }
  </style>

  </head>
  <body>
    <h2>  JavaScript Adding in HTML </h2>
    <p id="demo"> JavaScript can change the style of
an HTML element.</p>
    <script>
    function myFunction() {
        document.getElementById("demo").style.
fontSize = "25px";
        document.getElementById("demo").style.color
= "brown";
        document.getElementById("demo").style.
padding = "10px";
        document.getElementById("demo").style.
backgroundColor = "lightpink";
        document.getElementById("button").style.
backgroundColor = "lightgreen";
        document.getElementById("button").innerHTML
= "Visited";

    }
    </script>
    <button id="button" type="button"
onclick="myFunction()">Click Me!</button>
  </body>
    </html>
```

Here is another example of using JavaScript in HTML.

```
<!DOCTYPE html>
<html>
<head>
<style>
body{
  padding:10px;
```

```
  width:400px;
  margin:0 auto;
}
h1{
  text-align: center;
}
button{
  padding:20px;
  background-color: RGB(232, 111, 141);
  border: transparent;
  border-radius: 10px ;
}
.buttons{
  display: flex;
  justify-content: center;
  align-items: center;
}
</style>

</head>
<body>
  <h2>  JavaScript Adding in HTML </h2>
  <script>
    function light(img) {
        var pic;
        if (img == '0') {
            pic = "https://images.pexels.com/
photos/273003/pexels-photo-273003.jpeg?auto=compress&c
s=tinysrgb&w=400"
        } else {
            pic = "https://images.pexels.com/
photos/9801136/pexels-photo-9801136.jpeg?auto=compress
&cs=tinysrgb&w=400"
        }
        document.getElementById('myImage').src = pic;
    }
    </script>
    <img id="myImage" width="500"
height="300"  src="https://images.pexels.com/
photos/1922539/pexels-photo-1922539.jpeg?auto=compress
&cs=tinysrgb&w=400" width="100" height="180">
    <div class="buttons">
```

```
    <button type="button" onclick="light('1')"> Nature
image One</button>
    <button type="button" onclick="light('2')"> Nature
image Two </button>
    </p>
    </body>
  </html>
```

THE <noscript> ELEMENT

You can provide alternative info to the users whose web browsers do not support scripts and for those users who disabled the script option in their browsers. You can do this by using the <noscript> tag.

Example:

```
<noscript> Your browser does not support
JavaScript!</noscript>
```

Add the above line of code to know whether your browser supports JavaScript or not.

DEFAULT SCRIPTING LANGUAGE

There may be situations where you include multiple script files and end up using multiple <script> tags. You can specify a scripting language for all script tags. This saves you from having to specify the language every time you use a script tag on a page.

The example is given below.

```
<meta HTTP-Equiv = "Content-Script-Type" content =
"text/JavaScript" />
```

HTML AUDIO AND VIDEO

The HTML5 DOM has methods, properties, and events for the <audio> and <video> elements.

Methods

The HTML5 <audio> and <video> tags make it simple to add media to any website. You can set the src attribute to identify the media source and include a controls attribute so that the user can play and pause the media.

- addTextTrack(): It adds a new text track to the audio/video.

- canPlayType(): It checks whether the browser can play the specified audio/video type.

- load(): It re-loads the audio/video element.

- play(): It starts playing the audio/video.

- abort: It is generated when playback is aborted.

- canplay: It is generated when enough data is available that the media can be played.

- ended: It is generated when playback completes.

- error: It is generated when an error occurs.

- loaded data: It is generated when the first frame of the media has finished loading.

- loadstar: It is generated when loading of the media begins.

- pause: It is generated when playback is paused.

AUDIO AND VIDEO ATTRIBUTE

- autoplay

- autobuffer

- controls

- height

- loop

- preload

- poster

- src

- width

HTML HEAD ELEMENT

The <head> tag (element) is a container for the following elements such as <title>, <style>, <meta>, <link>, <script>, and <base>.[7] Let's discuss various tags that are usually added in the head section.

The <head> Element

The <head> is a container for metadata (that means data about data) that is placed between the <html> tag and the <body> tag.

The <title> Element

The <title> element defines the title of the HTML document. The title must be text-only; it is shown in the title browser bar or in the page's tab. The <title> element is required in the documents.

The <style> Element

The <style> element is used to describe style information for a single HTML page.

The <link> Element

The <link> element defines the relationship between the current document and an external resource.

CHAPTER SUMMARY

In the whole chapter, we discussed the various image attributes with their usage. You can also add favicon in your page. It is just a logo of your site. Besides that, we also discussed some audio and video attributes in the chapter. JavaScript plays an important role nowadays; to make your site attractive you need JavaScript. It also has various attributes and methods.

NOTES

1. HTML Favicon – https://www.digitalocean.com/community/tutorials/how-to-add-a-favicon-to-your-website-with-html, accessed on August 11, 2022.
2. HTML Picture Tag – https://www.geeksforgeeks.org/html-picture-tag/, accessed on August 13, 2022.
3. HTML Picture Tag – https://www.tutorialrepublic.com/html-tutorial/html-images.php, accessed on August 13, 2022.
4. HTML JavaScript – https://www.javatpoint.com/html-javascript, accessed on August 13, 2022.

5. HTML JavaScript – https://www.tutorialspoint.com/html/html_javascript. htm, accessed on August 13, 2022.
6. JavaScript HTML – https://www.taniarascia.com/understanding-events-in-javascript/, accessed on August 13, 2022.
7. HTML Head Element – https://www.w3schools.com/html/html_head.asp, accessed on August 13, 2022.

CHAPTER 6

HTML Tables

GETTING IN THIS CHAPTER

➢ HTML table

➢ HTML – Embed multimedia

➢ HTML Marquee

The previous chapter was of HTML image, favicon, JavaScript, embedded audio, and video. Here we will learn briefly about the Table, Embed multimedia, and Marquee with their attributes.

HTML TABLES

HTML tables allow the developers and web authors to organize data, such as text, images, links, other tables, etc., into rows and columns of cells. HTML tables are created by the <table> tag, whereas the <tr> tag is used to create table rows and the <td> tag is used to create data cells. Elements below <td> are normal and left-aligned by default.

Below are the different brands:

• <table>: It represents a table.

• <tr>: It represents a row in a table.

• <th>: It represents a header cell in a table.

• <td>: It represents a cell in a table.

DOI: 10.1201/9781003358077-6

- <caption>: It represents the caption of the table.

- <colgroup>: It represents a group of one or more columns in the table for formatting.

- <col>: It is used with the <colgroup> element to specify column properties for each column.

- <tbody>: It is used to group body content into a table.

- <thead>: It is used to group header content in a table.

- <footer>: It is used to group footer content into a table.

Example:

```
<!DOCTYPE html>
<html>
<head>
<style>
body {
  padding: 10px;
  width: 400px;
  margin: 0 auto;
}
h1 {
  text-align: center;
}
table {
  font-family: Arial, sans-serif;
  border-collapse: collapse;
  width: 100%;
}

td, th {
  border: 1px solid #dddddd;
  text-align: left;
  padding: 8px;
}

tr: nth-child(even) {
  background-color: #dddddd;
}
</style>

</head>
```

```
<body>
  <h2>  HTML Table Basic Example </h2>
  <table>
    <tr>
      <th> Name </th>
      <th> Age </th>
      <th> Country </th>
    </tr>
    <tr>
      <td> John </td>
      <td> 23 </td>
      <td> UK </td>
    </tr>
    <tr>
      <td> Sam </td>
      <td> 20 </td>
      <td> Mexico </td>
    </tr>
    <tr>
      <td> Lilly </td>
      <td> 15 </td>
      <td> Austrialia </td>
    </tr>
    <tr>
      <td> Sidhu </td>
      <td> 16 </td>
      <td> LA </td>
    </tr>
  </table>
  </body>
</html>
```

The output of the following code is given below.

Name	Age	Country
John	23	UK
Sam	20	Mexico
Lilly	15	Austrialia
Sidhu	16	LA

HTML table (basic structure).

\<th\> ELEMENTS

Now let's understand the table header cells that go at the start of a row or column and define the type of data that row or column contains.

TABLE CELLS

Each table cell is defined by a \<td\> and a \</td\> tags. The \<td\> stands for table data. You can write the content of the table cell between \<td\> and \</td\>.

Example:

```
<!DOCTYPE html>
<html>
<head>
<style>
<!DOCTYPE html>
<html>
<head>
<style>
body{
   padding:10px;
   width:400px;
   margin:0 auto;
}
h1{
   text-align: center;
}
table {
   font-family: Arial, sans-serif;
   border-collapse: collapse;
   width: 100%;
}

td, the {
   border: 1px solid #dddddd;
   text-align: left;
   padding: 8px;
}

tr:nth-child(even) {
```

```
   background-color: #dddddd;
}

</style>

</head>
<body>
  <h2>  HTML Table Adding CSS </h2>
  <table>
    <tr>
      <th> Name </th>
      <th> Age </th>
      <th> Country </th>
    </tr>
    <tr>
      <td> John </td>
      <td> 23 </td>
      <td> UK </td>
    </tr>
    <tr>
      <td> Sam </td>
      <td> 20 </td>
      <td> Mexico </td>
    </tr>
    <tr>
      <td> Lilly </td>
      <td> 15 </td>
      <td> Austrialia </td>
    </tr>
  </table>
    </body>
  </html>

</style>

</head>
<body>
  <h2> Table CSS </h2>

<table>
  <tr>
    <td> HTML </td>
```

```
    <td> CSS </td>
    <td> PHP </td>
  </tr>
  <tr>
    <td> HTML </td>
    <td> CSS </td>
    <td> PHP </td>
  </tr>
  <tr>
    <td> HTML </td>
    <td> CSS </td>
    <td> PHP </td>
  </tr>
</table>

    </body>
  </html>
```

The output of the following code is given below.

Name	Age	Country
John	23	UK
Sam	20	Mexico
Lilly	15	Austrialia

HTML table (adding CSS).

TABLE ROWS

Each table row starts with a <tr> tag and ends with a </tr> tag. The <tr> stands for table row.

Example:

```
<!DOCTYPE html>
<html>
<head>
<!DOCTYPE html>
<html>
```

```
<head>
<style>
body{
  padding:10px;
  width:400px;
  margin:0 auto;
}
h1{
  text-align: center;
}
table {
  font-family: Arial, sans-serif;
  border-collapse: collapse;
  width: 100%;
}

td, the {
  border: 1px solid #dddddd;
  text-align: left;
  padding: 8px;
}

tr:nth-child(even) {
  background-color: yellow;
}
tr:nth-child(odd) {
  background-color: greenyellow;
}
</style>

</head>
<body>
  <h2>  HTML Table Rows </h2>
  <table>
    <tr>
      <th> Name </th>
      <th> Age </th>
      <th> Country </th>
    </tr>
    <tr>
```

```
      <td> John </td>
      <td> 23 </td>
      <td> UK </td>
    </tr>
    <tr>
      <td> Sam </td>
      <td> 20 </t
      <td> Mexico </td>
    </tr>
    <tr>
      <td> Lilly </td>
      <td> 15 </td>
      <td> Austrialia </td>
    </tr>
  </table>
    </body>
  </html>
</head>
<body>
  <h2> Table CSS </h2>

<table>
  <tr>
    <td> HTML </td>
    <td> CSS </td>
    <td> PHP </td>
  </tr>
  <tr>
    <td> HTML </td>
    <td> CSS </td>
    <td> PHP </td>
  </tr>
  <tr>
    <td> HTML </td>
    <td> CSS </td>
    <td> PHP </td>
  </tr>
</table>

    </body>
  </html>
```

The output of the following code is given below.

Name	Age	Country
John	23	UK
Sam	20	Mexico
Lilly	15	Austrialia

HTML table (table rows).

You can have as many rows in a table, make sure that the number of cells is the same in each row.

HTML TABLE WITH BORDER

There are two methods to specify border for HTML tables:

- Using border attribute of table in HTML.

- Using border property in CSS.

TABLE HEADERS

The table header is defined as the <th> tag. The tag replaces the <td> tag that is used to represent the current data cell. You can place the top row as the table header; otherwise, you can use the <th> element on any row. Headings that are defined in the <th> tag are centered and bold by default.

Example:

```
<!DOCTYPE html>
<html>
<head>
<style>
body{
   padding:10px;
   width:400px;
   margin:0 auto;
}
```

```
h1{
  text-align: center;
}
table {
  font-family: Arial, sans-serif;
  border-collapse: collapse;
  width: 100%;
}

td, the {
  border: 1px solid #dddddd;
  text-align: left;
  padding: 8px;
}

th {
  background-color: yellow;
}
</style>

</head>
<body>
  <h2> HTML Table Header </h2>

  <table border = "1">
    <tr>
       <th> Name </th>
       <th> Age </th>
    </tr>
    <tr>
       <td> John </td>
       <td> 20 </td>
    </tr>

    <tr>
       <td> Sam </td>
       <td> 25 </td>
    </tr>
  </table>
    </body>
  </html>
```

The output of the following code is given below.

Name	Age
John	20
Sam	25

HTML table (table header).

Cellpadding AND Cellspacing ATTRIBUTES

There are two attributes known as cellpadding and cellspacing that you use to adjust the white space in table cells. The cellpacing attribute defines the space between table cells, while cellpadding represents the distance between the cell border and the content in the cell.

Example:

```
<!DOCTYPE html>
<html>
<head>
<style>

body{
   padding: 10px;
   width: 400px;
   margin:0 auto;
}
h1{
   text-align: center;
}
table {
   font-family: Arial, sans-serif;
   border-collapse: collapse;
   width: 100%;
}

td, the {
   border: 1px solid #dddddd;
   text-align: left;
   padding: 8px;
}
```

```
tr:nth-child( even) {
  background-color: #dddddd;
}
</style>

</head>
<body>
  <h2> HTML Table Header </h2>

<table border="1" cellpadding="4" cellspacing="5">
  <thead>
    <td>
      <span> Name </span>
    </td>
    <td>
      <span> Age </span>
    </td>
  </thead>
  <tbody>
  <tr>
    <td> Rani </td>
    <td> 30 </td>
  </tr>
  <tr>
    <td> Rajan </td>
    <td> 35 </td>
  </tr>
  <tr>
    <td> Akshaya </td>
    <td> 17 </td>
  </tr>
  <tr>
    <td> Ashick </td>
    <td> 13 </td>
  </tr>
  </tbody>
  </body>
</html>
```

Cellpadding

It specifies the defined space between the border of a table and its contents.[1] It defines the whitespace between the corners of the adjacent cells.

Syntax:

```
<table cellpadding = "value" > Add your code
</table>
```

Where, the value determines the padding (it is the space between the border of a table and its content).

Cellspacing

It specifies the space between cells. It defines the whitespace between the corners of the adjacent cells.

Syntax:

```
<table cellspacing = "value" > Code here </table>
```

Where, value determines the padding (it is space between adjacent cells).

Cellpadding AND Cellspacing DIFFERENCE

Cellpadding	Cellspacing
It is the space between the border of a table cell and its contents.	It is the space between adjacent cells.
The attribute is set to cellpadding.	The attribute is set to cell spacing.
It is for single cell.	It is for more than one cell.
The default value is 1.	The default value is 2.
It is widely used and effective.	It is less used and effective.

colspan AND rowspan ATTRIBUTES

You can use colspan attribute if you want to merge two or more columns into a single column. The similar way, you can use rowspan if you want to merge two or more rows.

Example:

```
<!DOCTYPE html>
<html>
<head>
<style>
```

```
body{
  padding: 10px;
  width: 400px;
  margin: 0 auto;
}
h1{
  text-align: center;
}
table {
  font-family: Arial, sans-serif;
  border-collapse: collapse;
  width: 100%;
}

td, the {
  border: 1px solid #dddddd;
  text-align: left;
  padding: 8px;
}

tr:nth-child(even) {
  background-color: #dddddd;
}
</style>

</head>
<body>
  <h2> HTML Table Header  </h2>

  <table border = "1">
    <tr>
       <th>Column 1</th>
       <th>Column 2</th>
       <th>Column 3</th>
    </tr>
    <tr>
       <td rowspan = "2"> Row 1 Cell 1 </td>
       <td> Row 1 Cell 2 </td>
       <td> Row 1 Cell 3 </td>
    </tr>
    <tr>
```

```
            <td> Row 2 Cell 2 </td>
            <td> Row 2 Cell 3 </td>
        </tr>
        <tr>
            <td colspan = "3"> Row 3 Cell 1 </td>
        </tr>
    </table>
    </body>
</html>
```

The output of the following code is given below.

Column 1	Column 2	Column 3
Row 1 Cell 1	Row 1 Cell 2	Row 1 Cell 3
	Row 2 Cell 2	Row 2 Cell 3
Row 3 Cell 1		

HTML table (rowspan and colspan).

TABLES BACKGROUNDS

There are two attributes of the table in HTML. You can set a background using one of the following two ways:

- bgcolor attribute – It can set a background color for the whole table or just for one cell.

- background attribute – It can set a background image for the whole table or just for one cell.

Example:

```
<!DOCTYPE html>
<html>
<head>
<style>
body{
    padding:10px;
    width:400px;
    margin:0 auto;
}
```

```
h1{
  text-align: center;
}
table {
  font-family: Arial, sans-serif;
}

td, the {
  border: 1px solid #dddddd;
  text-align: left;
  padding: 8px;
}

tr:nth-child(even) {
  background-color: #dddddd;
}
</style>

</head>
<body>
  <h2> HTML Table width and height  </h2>

  <table border = "1"  bordercolor = "green"
bgcolor = "lightgreen" width = "500" height =
"150">
    <tr>
       <th> Column 1 </th>
       <th> Column 2 </th>
       <th> Column 3 </th>
    </tr>
    <tr>
       <td rowspan = "2"> Row 1 Cell 1 </td>
       <td> Row 1 Cell 2 </td>
       <td> Row 1 Cell 3 </td>
    </tr>
    <tr>
       <td> Row 2 Cell 2 </td>
       <td> Row 2 Cell 3 </td>
    </tr>
    <tr>
       <td colspan = "3"> Row 3 Cell 1 </td>
    </tr>
```

```
  </table>
   </body>
</html>
```

The output of the following code is given below.

Column 1	Column 2	Column 3
Row 1 Cell 1	Row 1 Cell 2	Row 1 Cell 3
	Row 2 Cell 2	Row 2 Cell 3
Row 3 Cell 1		

HTML table (bgcolor and bordercolor).

You can also give an image as background using background attributes.

Example:

```
<!DOCTYPE html>
<html>
<head>
<style>
body{
  padding:10px;
  width:400px;
  margin:0 auto;
}
h1{
  text-align: center;
}
table {
  font-family: Arial, sans-serif;
}

td, the {
  border: 1px solid #dddddd;
  text-align: left;
  padding: 8px;
}

tr:nth-child(even) {
  background-color: #dddddd;
}
</style>
```

```
</head>
<body>
  <h2> HTML Table background  </h2>
  <table border = "1"  bordercolor = "green"
background="https://images.pexels.com/
photos/3408744/pexels-photo-3408744.jpeg?auto=comp
ress&cs=tinysrgb&w=400" bgcolor = "lightgreen"
width = "500" height = "150">
    <tr>
      <th> Column 1 </th>
      <th> Column 2 </th>
      <th> Column 3 </th>
    </tr>
    <tr>
      <td rowspan = "2"> Row 1 Cell 1 </td>
      <td> Row 1 Cell 2 </td>
      <td> Row 1 Cell 3 </td>
    </tr>
    <tr>
      <td> Row 2 Cell 2 </td>
      <td> Row 2 Cell 3 </td>
    </tr>
    <tr>
      <td colspan = "3"> Row 3 Cell 1 </td>
    </tr>
  </table>
  </body>
</html>
```

The output of the following code is given below.

Column 1	Column 2	Column 3
Row 1 Cell 1	Row 1 Cell 2	Row 1 Cell 3
	Row 2 Cell 2	Row 2 Cell 3
Row 3 Cell 1		

HTML table (background).

TABLE HEIGHT AND WIDTH

You can set the width and height of the table using the width and height attributes. You can specify the width or height of the table in pixels or as a percentage of the available screen area.

Example:

```
<!DOCTYPE html>
<html>
<head>
<style>
body{
  padding:10px;
  width:400px;
  margin:0 auto;
}
h1{
  text-align: center;
}
table {
  font-family: Arial, sans-serif;
}

td, the {
  border: 1px solid #dddddd;
  text-align: left;
  padding: 8px;
}

tr:nth-child(even) {
  background-color: #dddddd;
}

</style>

</head>
<body>
  <h2> HTML Table height and width  </h2>

  <table border = "1"  bordercolor = "green"
bgcolor = "lightgreen" width = "500" height = "150">
    <tr>
      <th> Column 1 </th>
```

```
        <th> Column 2 </th>
        <th> Column 3 </th>
    </tr>
    <tr>
        <td rowspan = "2"> Row 1 Cell 1 </td>
        <td> Row 1 Cell 2 </td>
        <td> Row 1 Cell 3 </td>
    </tr>
    <tr>
        <td> Row 2 Cell 2 </td>
        <td> Row 2 Cell 3 </td>
    </tr>
    <tr>
        <td colspan = "3"> Row 3 Cell 1 </td>
    </tr>
 </table>
  </body>
</html>
```

The output of the following code is given below.

Column 1	Column 2	Column 3
Row 1 Cell 1	Row 1 Cell 2	Row 1 Cell 3
	Row 2 Cell 2	Row 2 Cell 3
Row 3 Cell 1		

HTML table (height and width).

TABLE CAPTION

The caption tag is a title or explanation for the table and it shows up at the top of the table. Now, the tag is deprecated in newer version of HTML/ XHTML. Previously, the tag can automatically align the text in the center but not now.

Example:

```
<!DOCTYPE html>
<html>
<head>
```

```
<style>
body{
  padding:10px;
  width:400px;
  margin:0 auto;
}
h1{
  text-align: center;
}
table {
  font-family: Arial, sans-serif;
}

td, the {
  border: 1px solid #dddddd;
  text-align: left;
  padding: 8px;
}

tr:nth-child(even) {
  background-color: #dddddd;
}
</style>

</head>
<body>
  <h2> HTML Table width and height  </h2>
  <caption>This is the caption</caption>

  <table border = "1"  bordercolor = "green"
bgcolor = "light green" width = "500" height =
"150">
    <tr>
       <th>Column 1</th>
       <th>Column 2</th>
       <th>Column 3</th>
    </tr>
    <tr>
       <td rowspan = "2"> Row 1 Cell 1 </td>
       <td> Row 1 Cell 2 </td>
       <td> Row 1 Cell 3 </td>
    </tr>
```

```
      <tr>
         <td> Row 2 Cell 2 </td>
         <td> Row 2 Cell 3 </td>
      </tr>
      <tr>
         <td colspan = "3"> Row 3 Cell 1 </td>
      </tr>
   </table>
   </body>
</html>
```

The output of the following code is given below.

Column 1	Column 2	Column 3
	Row 1 Cell 2	Row 1 Cell 3
Row 1 Cell 1		
	Row 2 Cell 2	Row 2 Cell 3
Row 3 Cell 1		

HTML table (caption).

TABLE HEADER, BODY, AND FOOTER

Tables can be divided into three parts – head, body, and foot.[2] The header and footer are more like headers and footers in a word-processed document, which remain the same for each page, while the body is the main carrier of the table's content. Three elements separate the head, body, and foot of the table are:

- <thead> – It is used to create a separate table header. The <thead> element wraps up the part of the table that is the header; it is usually the very first row containing the column headers not always. If you use the <col>/<colgroup> element, the table header should be below them.

  Example:

```
<!DOCTYPE html>
<html>
<head>
```

```
<style>
body{
  padding:10px;
  width:400px;
  margin:0 auto;
}
h1{
  text-align: center;
}
table {
  font-family: Arial, sans-serif;
  border-collapse: collapse;
  width: 100%;
}

td, the {
  border: 1px solid #dddddd;
  text-align: left;
  padding: 8px;
}

tr:nth-child(even) {
  background-color: #dddddd;
}
</style>

</head>
<body>
  <h2> HTML Table thead  </h2>
  <table border = "1" width = "100%">
    <thead>
        <tr>
           <td colspan = "4"> Table Header </td>
        </tr>
    </thead>
 </table>
  </body>
</html>
```

- <tbody> – It is used to mark the body of the table. The <tbody> element needs to wrap up other parts of the table content that are not in the table header or footer. It appears below the table header.

Example:

```
<!DOCTYPE html>
<html>
<head>
<style>
body{
  padding:10px;
  width:400px;
  margin:0 auto;
}
h1{
  text-align: center;
}
table {
  font-family: Arial, sans-serif;
  border-collapse: collapse;
  width: 100%;
}

td, the {
  border: 1px solid #dddddd;
  text-align: left;
  padding: 8px;
}

tr:nth-child(even) {
  background-color: #dddddd;
}
</style>

</head>
<body>
  <h2> HTML Table tbody  </h2>
  <table border = "1" width = "100%">
    <tbody>
      <tr>
         <td> Cell 1 </td>
         <td> Cell 2 </td>
         <td> Cell 3 </td>
         <td> Cell 4 </td>
      </tr>
```

```
      </tbody>
   </table>
    </body>
</html>
```

- <tfoot> – It is used to create a separate table footer. The <tfoot> element wraps the part of the table that is the footer. You can include the
  table footer directly at the bottom of the table as you would expect,
  or directly below the table header.

Example:

```
<!DOCTYPE html>
<html>
<head>
<style>
body{
   padding:10px;
   width:400px;
   margin:0 auto;
}
h1{
   text-align: center;
}
table {
   font-family: Arial, sans-serif;
   border-collapse: collapse;
   width: 100%;
}

td, the {
   border: 1px solid #dddddd;
   text-align: left;
   padding: 8px;
}

tr:nth-child(even) {
   background-color: #dddddd;
}
</style>

</head>
```

```
<body>
  <h2> HTML Table tfoot  </h2>
  <table border = "1" width = "100%">
    <tfoot>
      <tr>
        <td colspan = "4"> Table Footer </td>
      </tr>
    </tfoot>


  </table>
  </body>
</html>
```

A table can contain several <tbody> elements to mark different pages or groups of data. However, it is noteworthy that <thead> and <tfoot> tags should appear before <tbody>.

Example:

```
<!DOCTYPE html>
<html>
<head>
<style>
body{
  padding:10px;
  width:400px;
  margin:0 auto;
}
h1{
  text-align: center;
}
table {
  font-family: Arial, sans-serif;
  border-collapse: collapse;
  width: 100%;
}

td, the {
  border: 1px solid #dddddd;
  text-align: left;
```

```
    padding: 8px;
}

tr:nth-child(even) {
  background-color: #dddddd;
}

tfoot{
  background-color: aqua;
}

tbody{
  background-color: yellow-green;
}

thead{
  background-color: royal blue;
}
</style>

</head>
<body>
  <h2> HTML Table thead, tbody, tfoot  </h2>
  <table border = "1" width = "100%">
    <thead>
      <tr>
        <td colspan = "4"> Table Header </td>
      </tr>
    </thead>

    <tbody>
      <tr>
        <td>Cell 1</td>
        <td>Cell 2</td>
        <td>Cell 3</td>
        <td>Cell 4</td>
      </tr>
    </tbody>

    <tfoot>
      <tr>
```

```
            <td colspan = "4"> Table Footer </td>
        </tr>
     </tfoot>


  </table>
   </body>
</html>
```

The output of the following code is given below.

Table Header			
Cell 1	Cell 2	Cell 3	Cell 4
Table Footer			

HTML table (thead, tfoot, and tbody).

NESTED TABLES

You can use a table inside another table, it is called nested.[3] But not only tables but you can use almost all the tags inside table data <td> tag.

Example:

```
<!DOCTYPE html>
<html>
<head>
<style>
body{
  padding:10px;
  width:400px;
  margin:0 auto;
}
h1{
  text-align: center;
}
table {
  font-family: Arial, sans-serif;
  width: 100%;
}
```

```
td, the {
  border: 1px solid #4e4040;
  text-align: left;
  padding: 8px;
}

tr:nth-child(even) {
  background-color: #dddddd;
}
</style>

</head>
<body>
  <h2> HTML Table nested  </h2>
  <table border = "1" width = "100%">

    <tr>
      <td>
        <table border = "1" width = "100%">
          <tr>
            <th> Column 1 </th>
            <th> Column 2 </th>
            <th> Column 3 </th>
          </tr>
          <tr>
            <td rowspan = "2"> Row 1 Cell 1 </td>
            <td> Row 1 Cell 2 </td>
            <td> Row 1 Cell 3 </td>
          </tr>
          <tr>
            <td> Row 2 Cell 2 </td>
            <td> Row 2 Cell 3 </td>
          </tr>
          <tr>
            <td colspan = "3"> Row 3 Cell 1 </td>
          </tr>
        </table>
      </td>
    </tr>
 </table>
  </body>
</html>
```

The output of the following code is given below.

Column 1	Column 2	Column 3
Row 1 Cell 1	Row 1 Cell 2	Row 1 Cell 3
	Row 2 Cell 2	Row 2 Cell 3
Row 3 Cell 1		

HTML table (nested tables).

STYLING WITH <col>

Instead of doing this, we can specify the information once on a <col> element. The <col> elements can be specified inside a <colgroup> container just below the opening <table> tag.

Example:

```
<!DOCTYPE html>
<html>
<head>
<style>
body{
  padding:10px;
  width:400px;
  margin:0 auto;
}
h1{
  text-align: center;
}
table {
  font-family: Arial, sans-serif;
  border-collapse: collapse;
  width: 100%;
}

td, the {
  border: 1px solid #dddddd;
```

```
   text-align: left;
   padding: 8px;
}

tr:nth-child(even) {
   background-color: #dddddd;
}
</style>

</head>
<body>
   <h2> HTML Table styling with colspan   </h2>
   <table border = "1" width = "100%">
     <thead>
        <tr>
           <td colspan = "4" style="background-
color: yellow"> Table Header </td>
        </tr>
     </thead>

     <tbody>
        <tr>
           <td> Cell 1 </td>
           <td> Cell 2 </td>
           <td> Cell 3 </td>
           <td> Cell 4 </td>
        </tr>
     </tbody>

     <tfoot>
       <tr>
         <td colspan = "4" style="background-
color: gray"> Table Footer </td>
       </tr>
    </tfoot>


 </table>
  </body>
</html>
```

The output of the following code is given below.

Table Header			
Cell 1	Cell 2	Cell 3	Cell 4
Table Footer			

HTML table (styling with colspan and rowspan).

THE scope ATTRIBUTE

The scope attribute can be added to the <th> element to tell screen readers exactly what cell the associated header is meant for.

Example:

```
<!DOCTYPE html>
<html>
<head>
<style>
body{
  padding:10px;
  width:400px;
  margin:0 auto;
}
h1{
  text-align: center;
}
table {
  font-family: Arial, sans-serif;
  width: 100%;
}

td, the {
  border: 1px solid black;
  text-align: left;
  padding: 8px;
}

tr:nth-child(even) {
  background-color: #dddddd;
}
</style>
```

```
  </head>
<body>
  <h2> HTML Nesting Tables  </h2>
  <table id="table1">
    <tr>
      <th  scope="col" > title1 </th>
      <th  scope="col" > title2 </th>
      <th  scope="col"> title3 </th>
    </tr>
    <tr>
      <td id="nested">
        <table id="table2">
          <tr>
            <td> cell1 </td>
            <td> cell2 </td>
            <td> cell3 </td>
          </tr>
        </table>
      </td>
      <td> cell2 </td>
      <td> cell3 </td>
    </tr>
    <tr>
      <td> cell4 </td>
      <td> cell5 </td>
      <td> cell6 </td>
    </tr>
  </table>
  </body>
</html>
```

The output of the following code is given below.

title1			title2	title3
cell1	cell2	cell3	cell2	cell3
cell4			cell5	cell6

HTML table (scope attributes).

ATTRIBUTES ID AND HEADERS

An alternative to the scope attribute is to use the id and headers attributes to create associations between headers and cells.[4] The way to use them is as follows.

You add a unique ID to each <th> element. You add the headers attribute to each <td> element. Each headers attribute must contain a space-separated list of IDs of all <th> elements that act as headers for that cell.

HTML TABLE SIZES

HTML tables can have various sizes for each column, row, or entire table. You can use the style attribute with the width and height properties to specify the size, row, or column of a table.

Example:

```
<!DOCTYPE html>
<html>
<head>
<style>
body{
  padding:10px;
  width:400px;
  margin:0 auto;
}
h1{
  text-align: center;
}
table {
  font-family: Arial, sans-serif;
  width: 100%;
}

td, the {
  border: 1px solid black;
  text-align: left;
  padding: 8px;
}
```

```
tr:nth-child(even) {
  background-color: #dddddd;
}
</style>

</head>
<body>
  <h2> HTML Table Width
  </h2>
  <table style="width: 100%">
    <tr>
      <th> First Name </th>
      <th> Last Name </th>
      <th> Age </th>
    </tr>
    <tr>
      <td> John </td>
      <td> Swift </td>
      <td> 26 </td>
    </tr>
    <tr>
      <td> Justin </td>
      <td> Click </td>
      <td> 28 </td>
    </tr>
  </table>
  </body>
</html>
```

The output of the following code is given below.

First Name	Last Name	Age
John	Swift	26
Justin	Clich	28

HTML table (table width).

HTML – EMBED MULTIMEDIA

Embedding Multimedia in HTML is adding images, audio, video, and other plugins to the web-using special HTML tags, the web browser started to support text and colors.[5] Multimedia has interactive content. Let's understand HTML Embed Multimedia in detail.

Embedded Multimedia

Multimedia elements are embedded in the documents by various methods, which are also used to add media files to an HTML web page supported by various types and formats.

There are three ways to add multimedia to the web page as given below:

1. HTML <embed> Tag

2. HTML <bgsound> Tag

3. HTML <object> Tag

The <embed> Tag

The <embed> tag is used to add multimedia files of external applications, which are mainly audio and video, and other plugins to a web page.

1. <embed> tag: Supported by most web browsers and new in HTML5.

2. <embed> tag: It only has an opening tag and does not guarantee to have a closing tag.

3. <noembed> tag: It is used when no web browser recognizes the HTML <embed> tag.

Syntax:

```
<embed src="URL">
```

The source (src) attribute is used to embed media into a document with the <embed> tag, and various media types are supported in <embed> elements. Here is an example of the <embed> text.

Example:

```
<!DOCTYPE html>
<html>
<head>
<style>
body{
  padding:10px;
  width:400px;
  margin:0 auto;
}
h1{
  text-align: center;
}
table {
  font-family: Arial, sans-serif;
  width: 100%;
}

td, the {
  border: 1px solid black;
  text-align: left;
  padding: 8px;
}

tr:nth-child(even) {
  background-color: #dddddd;
}
</style>

</head>
<body>
  <h2> HTML Embeded Multimedia ( embed tag )
</h2>
  <embed src="https://images.pexels.com/
photos/1781932/pexels-photo-1781932.jpeg?auto=comp
ress&cs=tinysrgb&w=400&lazy=load" height="400"
width="400"></embed>
  </body>
</html>
```

The output of the following code is given below.

HTML embedded (embed tag).

Here is an example of the <noembed> text.

```
<!DOCTYPE html>
<html>
<head>
<style>
body{
  padding:10px;
  width:400px;
  margin:0 auto;
}
h1{
  text-align: center;
}
</style>

</head>
<embed>
  <h2> HTML Embeded Multimedia ( noembed tag )</h2>
  <h4> It is Embeded </h4>
```

```
<embed src="https://images.pexels.com/
photos/13198286/pexels-photo-13198286.jpeg?auto=compre
ss&cs=tinysrgb&w=400&lazy=load" height="400"
width="400"> </embed>
  <h4> It is no Embeded </h4>
  <noembed>
    <img src="https://images.pexels.com/
photos/1781932/pexels-photo-1781932.jpeg?auto=compress
&cs=tinysrgb&w=400&lazy=load" height="400" width="400"
alt="Flower" />
  </noembed>
  </body>
</html>
```

The output of the following code is given below.

It is Embeded

It is no Embeded

HTML embedded (noembed tag).

Here is an example of the <object> text.

```
<!DOCTYPE html>
<html>
```

```
<head>
<style>
body{
  padding:10px;
  width:400px;
  margin:0 auto;
}
h1{
  text-align: center;
}
table {
  font-family: Arial, sans-serif;
  width: 100%;
}

td, the {
  border: 1px solid black;
  text-align: left;
  padding: 8px;
}

tr:nth-child(even) {
  background-color: #dddddd;
}
</style>

</head>
<embed>
  <h2> HTML Embeded Multimedia ( object tag )</h2>
  <object data="" > When the data is not provided this
text will be shown </object>
  <h4> It is object tag </h4>
    <object data=
  "https://images.pexels.com/photos/1781932/pexels-
photo-1781932.jpeg?auto=compress&cs=tinysrgb&w=400&laz
y=load" height="400" width="400" alt="Flower""
        width="550px" height="150px"> Here you can
provide information about the object </object>
  </body>
</html>
```

The output of the following code is given below.

When the data is not provided this text will be shown

It is object tag

HTML embedded (object tag).

Supported Video Types

You can use different types of media in the embed tag, such as Flash movies (.swf), AVI files (.avi), and MOV files (.mov).

- .swf files – These files are file types created by Macromedia's Flash program.

- .wmv files – These files are Microsoft's Media Video file types.

- .mov files – These files are in Apple's Quick Time Movie format.

- .mpeg files – These files are movie files created by the Moving Pictures Expert Group.

The following is a list of important attributes that can be used with the <embed> tag. The most common attributes used by an element to add multimedia to HTML are listed below:

- height: It defines the height of the multimedia object in pixels.

- src: It defines the web browser URL as an embedded media object.

- width: It defines the width of the multimedia object in pixels.

- type: It is used to define the media type of the built-in plug-in.

- name: It is used to define the reference of the object.

- volume: It is used to control volume of the sound. Can be from 0 (off) to 100 (full volume).

The <bgsound> Tag

You can use the <bgsound> HTML tag to play an audio track in the background of your web page. Only Internet Explorer supports this tag, and most other browsers ignore this tag. When a user first downloads and displays a host document, it downloads and plays an audio file. The background audio file will also play whenever the user refreshes the browser.

Points to remember:

- <bgsound> tag: In an HTML document, it is used to add background sound media to a web page.

- <bgsound> tag: Mainly used in Internet Explorer and ignored by most browsers. It is deprecated from the latest version of HTML.

- <bgsound> tag: It is used when playing background sound repeatedly whenever the browser refreshes the HTML document.

- <audio> tag: It is used in the latest version of HTML instead of the <bgsound> tag.

- <bgsound> tag: It does not display any content, but only the accompanying sound in the HTML document.

There are two main attributes used in the <bgsound> element to add background sound:

- loop – It defines how many times the background sound will be played in a loop with specified conditions.

- src – It defines the URL path to the embedded audio track.

The <object> Tag

HTML 4 introduces the <object> element, which offers a universal solution for embedding generic objects. The <object> element allows HTML authors to specify everything an object requires to be presented by a user agent. The <object> tag is used to add external object multimedia files, which are mainly audio, images, pdf, flash, video, and other web pages to the current web page.

- The <object> tag is supported by web browsers. It was introduced in HTML 4.

- The <object> element is defined in the <body> tag of an HTML document.

- The <param> tag is used as plugin parameters that have been included with the <object> tag.

- An HTML document object can be defined under the <object> tag of the current HTML document.

Syntax:

```
<object type=""> </object> or <object data=""> </object>
```

Attributes of the <object> tag

Common attributes used in the <object> element to add multimedia to HTML:

- height: It defines the height of the multimedia object in pixels.

- form: It defines the form ID of the object element.

- width: It defines the width of the multimedia object in pixels.

- type: It defines the media type of the embedded plug-in.

HTML MARQUEE

The Marquee Element in HTML is used to handle the effect of scrolling text and images in different directions using attributes on a web page of an HTML document to improve the appearance of the web.[6]

Usage

The HTML <marquee> tag is a container tag used to define the scrolling effect of a text or image element vertically or horizontally, or more precisely, the scrolling of the element is either top to bottom or left to right or vice versa.

The <marquee> tag is used in HTML 4 and is no longer used in the latest version of HTML, i.e. HTML5. Instead of the <marquee> tag, Javascript and cascading styles are used for the same effects.

The <marquee> tag supports global and event attributes and is only supported by a few browsers, e.g. firefox, internet explorer, safari, chrome, etc. A <marquee> tag starts with an opening tag and ends with a closing tag with the attribute value and content in between.

Syntax:

```
<marquee attribute name = "marquee attribute
value..."> content </marquee>
```

Example:

```
<!DOCTYPE html>
<html>
<head>
<style>
body{
   padding:10px;
   width:680px;
   margin:0 auto;
}
h1{
   text-align: center;
}
p{
   font-size:20px
```

```
}
</style>

</head>
<embed>
  <h1> HTML Marquee tag </h1>
  <marquee> <p> Lorem ipsum dolor sit amet,
consectetur adipiscing elit. In viverra nunc non
diam faucibus, non cursus metus elementum.
Vestibulum vel sapien sapien. Ut a est viverra,
tempus metus sed, lacinia mi. Suspendisse potenti.
</p> </marquee>
</body>
</html>
```

The output of the following code is given below.

Lorem ipsum dolor sit amet, consectetur adipiscing elit. In

HTML Marquee (basic example)

ATTRIBUTES IN <marquee> TAG

There are several attributes of <marquee> tag in HTML that are given below:

Attributes	Description
behaviour	This attribute is used to define the type of scrolling in the frame with values like slide, scroll, and alternative.
direction	This attribute is used to define the scrolling direction with a value of up, down, right, and left.
width:	This attribute is used to define the width of the selection in pixels or percentages.
height:	This attribute is used to define the height of the selection in pixels or percentages.
scroll delay	This attribute is used to define the delay between scrolls in milliseconds.
scroll amount:	This attribute is used to define an interval in the selection speed in numbers.
Loop	This attribute is used to define the number of times to scroll the frame in number, the default number is infinite.
Vspace	This attribute is used to define the vertical space around the frame with a value in pixels.
Hspace	This attribute is used to define the horizontal space around the frame with a value in pixels.

Let's discuss the above-listed attributes one by one.

1. behavior marquee attribute: The marquee behavior attribute is used to set the scrolling behavior. The default value is scroll.

   Syntax:

   ```
   <markquee behavior=slide>
   ```

   This attribute has a variable value:

   - alternate: It defines that the text moves to the end and then starts in the opposite direction.

   - scroll: It has a default value. It specifies that the text moves to the end and starts again.

   - frame: It sets the text to move to the end and then stops it.

   Example:

   ```
   <!DOCTYPE html>
   <html>
   <head>
   <style>
   body{
     padding:10px;
     width:680px;
     margin:0 auto;
   }

   h1{
     text-align: center;
   }
   p{
     font-size:24px

   }
   marquee{
     padding:20px;
     margin:10px;
     background-color: lightcoral;
   }
   </style>
   ```

```
</head>
<embed>
  <h1> HTML Marquee tag (behavior attribute)
</h1>
  <marquee class= "marq"
  direction= "left"
  behavior= scroll
  loop= "">
<p> Srolling text </p>
</marquee>
<marquee class=" marq"
  behavior= alternate
  direction= "left"
  loop= "" >
  <p> Alternate text (left) </p>
</marquee>
</body>
</html>
```

The output of the following code is given below.

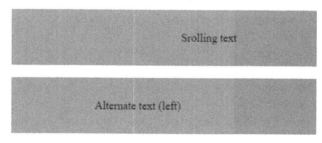

HTML Marquee (behavior attribute).

2. scroll delay marquee attribute: The Marquee scroll delay attribute in HTML is used to set the interval between each scrolling movement in milliseconds. The default Scrolldelay value is 85.

Syntax:

```
<marquee scrolldelay=number>
```

Another value:

• number: It defines the selection speed.

Example:

```
<!DOCTYPE html>
<html>
<head>
<style>
body{
  padding:10px;
  width:680px;
  margin:0 auto;
}
h1{
  text-align: center;
}
p{
  font-size:24px

}
marquee{
  padding:20px;
  margin:10px;
  background-color: lightcoral;
}
</style>

</head>
<embed>
  <h1> HTML Marquee tag (behavior attribute)
</h1>
  <marquee class= "marq"
  direction= "left"
  behavior= scroll
  loop= "">
<p> Scrolldelay text (normal) </p>
</marquee>
<marquee class=" marq"
  Scrolldelay=200
  direction="left"
  loop= "" >
  <p> Scrolldelay text (100) </p>
</marquee>
<marquee class=" marq"
```

```
Scrolldelay=800
direction="left"
loop= "" >
<p> Scrolldelay text (800) </p>
</marquee>
</body>
</html>
```

The output of the following code is given below.

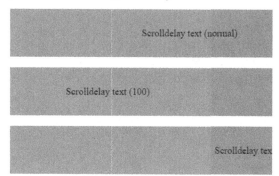

HTML Marquee (scroll delay attribute).

3. loop marquee attribute: The selection loop attribute in HTML is used to define the amount of time a selection box should repeat. The default loop value is INFINITE.

Syntax:

```
<marquee loop="number" >
```

Another value,

- number: It defines the selection speed.

Example:

```
<!DOCTYPE html>
<html>
<head>
<style>
body{
  padding:10px;
```

```
  width:680px;
  margin:0 auto;
}
h1{
  text-align: center;
}
p{
  font-size:24px

}
marquee{
  padding:20px;
  margin:10px;
  background-color: lightcoral;
}
</style>

</head>
<embed>
  <h1> HTML Marquee tag (loop attribute) </h1>
  <marquee class= "marq"
  direction= "left"
  behavior= scroll
  loop= "">
<p> Loop = "" </p>
</marquee>
<marquee class=" marq"
  Scrolldelay=200
  direction="left"
  loop= "2" >
  <p>  Loop = "2"  </p>
</marquee>
<marquee class=" marq"
  Scrolldelay=800
  direction="left"
  loop= "5" >
  <p> Loop = "5" </p>
</marquee>
</body>
</html>
```

The output of the following code is given below.

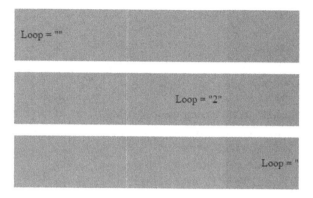

HTML Marquee (loop attribute).

4. bgcolor marquee attribute: The Marquee bgcolor attribute in HTML is used to set the background color of the marquee. Now, it is not supported in HTML5.

Attribute value:

- color name: It defines the background color of the marquee.

Example:

```
<!DOCTYPE html>
<html>
<head>
<style>
body{
   padding:10px;
   width:680px;
   margin:0 auto;
}

h1{
   text-align: center;
}
p{
   font-size:24px
}
```

```
marquee{
  padding:20px;
  margin:10px;
}
</style>

</head>
<embed>
  <h1> HTML Marquee tag (bgcolor attribute) </h1>
  <marquee class= "marq"
  direction= "left"
  behavior= scroll
  bgcolor="light green"
  loop= "">
<p>  bgcolor="light cyan"
</p>
</marquee>
<marquee class=" marq"
  Scrolldelay=200
  bgcolor="light yellow"
  direction="left"
  loop= "2" >
  <p>   bgcolor="light yellow"
  </p>
</marquee>
<marquee class=" marq"
  Scrolldelay=800
  bgcolor="light cyan"
  direction="left"
  loop= "5" >
  <p>   bgcolor="light cyan"
  </p>
</marquee>
</body>
</html>
```

The output of the following code is given below.

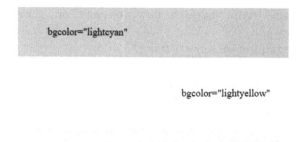

HTML Marquee (bgcolor attribute).

5. direction marquee attribute: The Marquee direction attribute is used to set the direction of the text of marquee.

Example:

```
<!DOCTYPE html>
<html>
<head>
<style>
body{
   padding:10px;
   width:680px;
   margin:0 auto;
}

h1{
   text-align: center;
}
p{
   font-size:24px

}
marquee{
   padding:20px;
   margin:10px;
}
</style>
```

```
</head>
<embed>
  <h1> HTML Marquee tag (direction attribute)
</h1>
  <marquee class= "marq"
  direction= "left"
  behavior= scroll
  bgcolor="light cyan"
  loop= "">
<p>  direction (left)
</p>
</marquee>
<marquee class=" marq"
  bgcolor="light cyan"
  direction="up"
  loop= "" >
  <p>    direction (up)
  </p>
</marquee>
<marquee class=" marq"
  bgcolor="light cyan"
  direction="down"
  loop= "" >
  <p>    direction (down)
  </p>
</marquee>
<marquee class=" marq"
  bgcolor="light cyan"
  direction="right"
  loop= "" >
  <p>    direction (right)
  </p>
</marquee>
</body>
</html>
```

The output of the following code is given below.

direction (left)

direction (down)

direction (right)

HTML Marquee (direction attribute).

6. width marquee attribute: The Marquee direction attribute is used to set the width of the text of marquee.

Example:

```
<!DOCTYPE html>
<html>
<head>
<style>
body{
  padding:10px;
  width:680px;
  margin:0 auto;
}

h1{
  text-align: center;
}
p{
  font-size:24px

}
marquee{
  padding:20px;
```

```
    margin:10px;
}
</style>

</head>
<embed>
    <h1> HTML Marquee tag (width attribute) </h1>
    <marquee class= "marq"
    direction= "left"
    bgcolor="light green"
    behavior= scroll
    width = "50%"
        loop= "">
<p>  width (50%)
</p>
</marquee>
<marquee class=" marq"
    bgcolor="light cyan"
    width = "100%"
    loop= "" >
    <p>     width (100%)
    </p>
</marquee>
</body>
</html>
```

The output of the following code is given below.

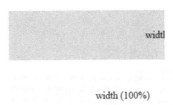

width (100%)

HTML Marquee (width attribute).

SCROLLING SPEED

Marquee speed can help to change the "scrollmount" attribute.[7] For example, if using scrollmount = "1" then it sets the marque to scroll very slowly, as you increase the "scrollmount", the scrolling speed will also increase. For example, scrollamount= "100".

Example:

```
<!DOCTYPE html>
<html>
<head>
<style>
body{
   padding:10px;
   width:680px;
   margin:0 auto;
}
h1{
   text-align: center;
}
p{
   font-size:24px

}
marquee{
   padding:20px;
   margin:10px;
}
</style>

</head>
<embed>
   <h1> HTML Marquee tag ( Scrolling Speed ) </h1>
   <marquee behavior="scroll" direction="up"
scrollamount="1">Slow Scrolling</marquee>
   <marquee behavior="scroll" direction="right"
scrollamount="12">Little Fast Scrolling</marquee>
   <marquee behavior="scroll" direction="left"
scrollamount="20">Fast Scrolling</marquee>
   <marquee behavior="scroll" direction="right"
scrollamount="50">Very Fast Scrolling</marquee>
</body>
</html>
```

The output of the following code is given below.

Slow Scrolling

Little Fast Scrolling

Scrolling

Very

HTML Marquee (scrolling speed).

BLINK TEXT

In the Marquee, you can also define the blinker using keyframes in the CSS to apply to your content. Here is an example of the blink text.

Example:

```
<!DOCTYPE html>
<html>
<head>
<style>
body{
  padding:10px;
  width:680px;
  margin:0 auto;
}
h1{

  text-align: center;
}
p{
  font-size:24px

}
marquee{
  padding:20px;
  margin:10px;
}
```

```
.blink_1 {
        animation: blinker 1.5s linear
infinite;
        color: red;
        font-family: sans-serif;
    }
    @keyframes blinker {
        50% {
            opacity: 0;
        }
    }

</style>

</head>
<embed>
  <h1> HTML Marquee tag ( blinker ) </h1>
<marquee class="blink_1"> This is an example of
blinking text using CSS within a marquee.
</marquee>
</body>
</html>
```

The output of the following code is given below.

This is an example of blinking text using CSS within a marquee.

HTML Marquee (blinker).

CHAPTER SUMMARY

In this chapter, we discussed table with their various tags that are generally used inside the <table> such as <tr>, <th>, <thead>, <tbody, <tfoot>, and <td>, with their attributes along with the Ended multimedia attributes with their attributes. Besides that, you got the explanation of the marquee tag. Our next chapter is of HTML forms.

NOTES

1. HTML Table (cellpadding and cellspacing) – https://www.geeksforgeeks.org/difference-between-cellpadding-and-cellspacing/, accessed on August 15, 2022.

2. HTML Table header, body and footer – https://www.tutorialspoint.com/html/html_tables.htm, accessed on August 15, 2022.

3. HTML Tested Table – https://developer.mozilla.org/en-US/docs/Learn/HTML/Tables/Advanced, accessed on August 15, 2022.

4. HTML Attributes – https://developer.mozilla.org/en-US/docs/Learn/HTML/Tables/Advanced#nesting_tables, accessed on August 15, 2022.

5. HTML Multimedia – https://www.tutorialspoint.com/html/html_embed_multimedia.htm, accessed on August 16, 2022.

6. HTML Marquee – https://codedec.com/tutorials/marquee-tag-in-html/, accessed on August 16, 2022.

7. HTML Marquee tags – https://www.w3schools.in/html/marquee-tag, accessed on August 16, 2022.

HTML Forms

GETTING IN THIS CHAPTER

➤ HTML Forms

➤ HTML input form Attribute

➤ HTML input Attribute

In the previous chapter, we discussed various topics of HTML such as Table, Marquee, and Multimedia with their attributes. Now, this chapter covers styling a web form that requests various data from the user. The form can use text fields, radio buttons, checkboxes, drop-downs, a textarea, and submit and reset buttons. The forms are basically a very important part of any website. It is a way to take user's information and process requests. Web forms are a basic element of website design, ranging from the complex of a search form to contact forms and complex data filtering.

HTML FORMS

Forms offer controls for every application use. Using the form controls and form fields, we can request small and large amounts of information such as user ID, password, billing details, job application, etc. You can create and modify form and its elements by resetting styles using the appearance property, setting own consistent style for the form, adding placeholder responses for text fields, and customizing radio buttons and checkboxes using other pseudo-classes and pseudo-elements.

DOI: 10.1201/9781003358077-7

Now, first add up the basic HTML and CSS for forms then save this file with index.html page. Begin by opening the index.html file in the editor. Then, add the following HTML code to provide a base structure for the file.

```
<!doctype html>
<html>
  <head>
    <meta charset="utf-8">
    <meta content="width=device-width,
name="viewport" initial-scale=1">
    <title>CSS Form</title>
    <link rel="stylesheet" href="styles.css" />
  </head>
  <body>
    <main>

    <!-- Write your code -->

    </main>
  </body>
</html>
```

The elements contained in the <head> define the title of the page with the <title> tag where to load the stylesheet using the <link> element. <meta> tags define the character encoding and guide the browser on how to display the website on a small-screen device. The content of the main form will be placed inside the <body> and <main> tags.

Next, in the <main> tag, create a <form> element. Inside the <form> you add various form elements and <div> elements to help with the layout. This tutorial highlights the additions to the code from the previous steps. Add the highlighted HTML from the following block of code to the index. html file.

BASIC STRUCTURE OF FORMS IN CSS

In order to get information through a form, we must first learn how to create it.[1] The syntax is shown below.

```
<form action="URL" method="post">
    /* form inputs*/
    </form>
```

To add a form to a web page, we need to add a <form> element. All input fields and form controls should be wrapped in a <form> element. There are many attributes available for a form element, but the most used or important ones are action and method.

HTML FORM TAGS

Let's check the list of HTML5 form tags listed below:

- <form> defines an HTML form for entering inputs on the used page.
  The <form> tag defines a form that contains attractive controls that allow a user to submit information to a web server. An HTML form is used to capture other information such as name, password, address, email details, credit card information, and so on.

  Information can be captured in a form using many different form controls such as <input>, <textarea>, <select>, <option>, and <button>. There are also labeling and grouping controls that include the <optgroup>, <fieldset>, <legend>, and <label> elements.

- <input> defines an input control.
  The HTML <input> element is the used form element. An <input> element can display in many ways, depending on the type attribute: <input type="text"> displays a single-line text input field, <input type="radio"> displays a radio button, <input type="checkbox"> displays a checkbox, <input type="submit"> displays a submit button, and <input type="button"> displays a clickable button.

  Text fields are used to gather information from the user. It can be created using the <input> element and its type attribute, which describes what type of information we want the user to enter. We can set the name of the input element using the name attribute.

  Here is the syntax of text fields,

```
<input type="text" name="name">
```

- <textarea> defines a multiline input control.
  The text area is only used to receive text information. A text area field can be created using the <textarea> element. This element cannot accept a type attribute because it only accepts one type of value, but it does accept a name attribute, which means that the user can name the text field.

Here is the syntax of text area,

```
<textarea name="comment">Add your text here.
</textarea>
```

- <label> defines a label for the input element.

  Labels are used to give captions or headings to form controls. Labels are created using the <label> element. It is considered better to have a label in the form. If you click on the label, it will focus on the text control. To do so, you must have a form attribute on the label tag that must be the same as the input tag's id attribute.

  Example:

- <fieldset> groups a related element into a form.

  The text area is only used to receive text information. A text area field can be created using the <textarea> element. This element cannot accept a type attribute because it only accepts one type of value, but it does accept a name attribute, which means that the user can name the text field.

- <legend> defines a legend for the <fieldset> element.

  A legend is used to provide a form header that gives a quick idea of the type of form. The legend is created using the <legend> element immediately after the opening <fieldset> element.

  Here is the syntax,

```
<fieldset>
    <legend>Login form</legend>
    <label for="username"> Username
    <input type="text" name="username">
    </label>
    <label for="password"> Password
    <input type="text" name="password">
    </label>
</fieldset>
```

- <select> defines a drop-down list.

  The <select> is used to create a drop-down list. It is often used in a form to collect user input. The name attribute is needed to have a reference of form data after the form is submitted. Here the id is needed to associate the drop-down list with a label. There are various attributes used in <select> tag such as autofocus, disabled, form, multiple, and required.

Example:

```
<select name="cars" id="cars">
    <option value="HTML"> HTML </option>
    <option value="CSS "> CSS </option>
    <option value="PHP">PHP </option>
  </select>
```

• <optgroup> defines an optgroup of related various options in a drop-down list.

The <optgroup> tag is used to group related options in a <select> element (drop-down list). There are various attributes of optgroup such as disabled and label.

Example:

```
<select name="cars" id="cars">
    <optgroup  value="HTML"> HTML </optgroup>
    <optgroup  value="CSS "> CSS </optgroup>
    <optgroup  value="PHP">PHP </optgroup>
  </select>
```

• <option> defines the option in the drop-down list.
Also the <option> tag defines an option in a select list. Its elements go inside a <select>, <optgroup>, or <datalist> element. The <option> element helps to define an item contained in a <select>. The <option> can represent menu items in popups and other lists of items in a document.

Example:

```
<select name="cars" id="cars">
    <option value="HTML"> HTML </option>
    <option value="CSS "> CSS </option>
    <option value="PHP">PHP </option>
  </select>
```

- <button> defines a clickable button.
  It is used to specify the one or more forms that the <button> element belongs to. The <button> tag defines a clickable button. It is used inside a <button> element you can put text tags like <i>, <b>, <strong>, <br>, <img>, etc.

  Example:

  ```
  <button > Submit </button>
  ```

- <checkbox>
  The checkbox is a square box that is ticked (checked) when activated. These are used to let a user select more than one option of a limited number of choices.
  Here is the syntax of <checkbox>,

  ```
  <input type="checkbox">
  ```

  Example:

  ```
  <input type="checkbox" value="HTML">
  ```

- <radio>
  Radio buttons are presented in radio groups. Basically, it is a collection of radio buttons describing a set of related options. The only radio button in a group can be selected at the same time.
  Here is the syntax of radio,

  ```
  <input type="radio">
  ```

  Example:

  ```
  <input type="radio" value="HTML">
  ```

VARIOUS FORM ATTRIBUTES

Below are the various form attributes that you can use in your code:

- action: The backend script is ready to process your passed data. The action attribute defines the action to be performed when the form is submitted. The data is sent to a file on the server when the user clicks on the submit button. In the example, the form data is sent to a file called "actione_page.php". The file contains a server-side script that handles the form data.

- method: The method to use to upload the data. The method attribute specifies the HTTP method to use when submitting form data. Form data can be submitted as a URL variable (with method= "get") or as an HTTP post transaction (with method= "post").

The two common methods for the request-response between a server and client are[2]:

1. GET – It requests the data from a specified resource.

2. POST – It submits the processed data to a specified resource.

The GET method refers to the HyperText Transfer Protocol (HTTP) method used to request information from a particular resource. It is also used to specific variables derived from a group. The POST HTTP requests information from the supplying browser to be inserted into the server's message system.

KEY DIFFERENCES

GET	POST
The parameters maintain in the server since it forms a portion of the URL.	The parameters do not remain since it is not within the browser history.
It is capable of being bookmarked since it is within the URL.	It cannot be bookmarked.
The GET method of HTTP sends parameter information but with a limitation to what is acceptable to the URL.	The POST method of HTTP sends information to the server without any kind of problem, including the information in the user form of uploaded files.
The URL is limited to 2000 characters under the GET method.	It method does not feature such restrictions.
The GET method is easily get with this not safe since the information received is saved in the URL, which means that anyone else can have access to it.	On the other side, the POST method is safer but not easily cracked up. The POST parameters are not maintained on the server or webpages, thus it is not easily accessed.

- target: This attribute specifies where to display the result that is received after submitting the form. It also specifies the target window or frame where the script result will be displayed. It takes values such as _blank, _self, _parent, etc.

Here is the explanation of the target values:

1. _blank: The answer will be dispayed in a new window or tab.

2. _self: The answer will be displayed in the current window.

3. _parent: The response will be displayed in the parent frame.

4. _top: The answer will be displayed in the entire body of the window.

5. framename: The response will be displayed in the named iframe.

6. enctype: User can use the enctype attribute to specify how the browser performs and encodes data before sending it to the server. The possible values are:

   - application/x-www-form-urlencoded – It is the standard method that most forms use in simple scenarios.

   - multipart/form-data – It is used when you want to upload binary data in the form of files like image, word file, etc.

HTML FORM CONTROLS

There are various types of form controls that you can use to collect data using HTML form such as[3]:

- Text Input Controls: In the text control, there are also more categories such as Single-line text input controls, Password input controls, Multiple-line text input controls, etc.

There are three types of text input used in forms:

1. Single Line Text Input Controls – It is used for items that require only one line of user input such as search fields or titles. They are created using the HTML <input> tag.

Example:

```
<form action="index.php" method="GET">
    First name:
    <input type="text" name="First name" />
    <br>
    Last name:
    <input type="text" name="Last name" />
    <input type="submit" value="submit" />
</form>
```

The following is a list of attributes for the <input> tag:

- type: It indicates the type of input control you want to create. This element is used to create other form controls such as radio buttons and checkboxes.

- name: It is used to specify the name of the part of the name/value pair that is sent to the server representing each form control and value that the user entered.

- value: It provides the initial value for the text input control that the user will see when the form is loaded.

- size: It allows you to specify the width of the text input control in characters.

- maxlength: It allows you to specify the maximum number of characters that the user can enter in the text field.

2. Password Entry Controls – It is single-line text input, but masks the character once the user has entered it. They are created using the HTML <input> tag.

   The following is a list of attributes for the <input> tag to create a password field.

   - type: It indicates the input control type and will be set to password for password input control.

   - name: It is used to specify the name of the control that is sent to the server to be recognized and get a value.

   - value: This can be used to specify an initial value inside the control.

- size: It allows to specify the width of the text input control in characters.

- maxlength: It allows you to specify the maximum number of characters that the user can enter in the text field.

3. Multiline Text Entry Controls – It is used when the user is required to enter details that may be longer than one sentence. Multiline input controls are created using the <textarea> HTML tag.
   Here is the following list of attributes for <textarea> tag:

- name: It is used to specify the name of the control that is sent to the server to be recognized and get a value.

- rows: It indicates the number of lines of the text field.

- cols: it indicates the number of columns of the text field.

- Checkboxes Controls – Checkboxes are used when more than one option is required to be selected. They are created by using the HTML <input> tag, but the type attribute is set to checkbox.

  Following is the list of attributes for < checkboxes > tag:

  1. type: It indicates the type of input control and for checkbox input control. It will set to checkbox.

  2. name: Used to specify the name of the control that is sent to the server to be recognized and get a value.

  3. value: The value will be used if the box is checked.

  4. checked: It sets to checked if you want to select it by default.

- Radio Box Controls – A radio button is used to select one of many given options.[4] The radio buttons are displayed in radio button groups to show a set of related options from which only one can be selected. A radio in HTML can be defined using the <input> tag.
  The general syntax for a radio definition is:

```
<input type="radio" name="and"...>
```

The following is a list of important attributes of the <radio> tag:

1. type: The type attribute of the input tag. When creating a radio button, it must be "radio", but it can be other input types, such as button, checkbox, file, etc.

2. name: It specifies the name of the input element. Switches with the same name form a switch group.

3. value: The value against the radio button that, if checked, is sent to the server.

Here are some examples using attributes for radio buttons such as:

1. Checked radio button

2. Disabled radio button

- Select Box Controls – A selection box, also called a drop-down box, that provides the ability to list various options in the form of a drop-down list from which the user can select one or more options.
  The following is a list of important attributes of the <select> tag:

1. name: It is used to specify the name of the control that is sent to the server to be recognized and get a value.

2. size: It can be used to display a scrolling list.

3. more: If set to "more", it allows the user to select more items from the menu.

In the <select> tag, we have one more tag known as <option>:

1. value: The value that is used if an option is selected in the select field.

2. selected: It specifies that the option should be the initially selected value on page load.

3. label: An alternative way of labeling.

- Hidden Controls – Hidden form controls are used to hide data inside a page that can later be sent to the server. This control is hidden inside the code and does not appear on the actual page. For example, the following hidden form is used to preserve the current page number. When the user clicks on the next page, the value of the hidden control will be sent to the web server and it will decide which page to display next based on the current page passed.

- Control buttons – There are different ways to create clickable buttons in HTML.[5] You can create a clickable button using the <input> tag by setting its type attribute to button. The type attribute can take on the following values –

  The following is a list of important attributes of the <button> tag:

  1. submit: This will create a button that will automatically submit the form.

  2. reset: It can create a button that automatically resets the form controls to their default values.

  3. button: It can create a button that is used to run a client-side script when the user clicks on the button.

  4. image: This will create a clickable button, but we can use an image as the background of the button.

- File upload field

  If a user wants to upload a file to a website, you will need to use a file upload field, also known as a file selection field. It is also created using the <input> element, but the type attribute is set to file.
  The following is a list of important file upload field attributes:

  1. name: It is used to specify the name of the control that is sent to the server to be recognized and get a value.

  2. accept: It specifies the file types that the server accepts.

HTML FORM INPUT TYPES

In HTML, the <input type=" "> is an element of HTML form.[6] The "type" attribute of the input element can be of other types that define the information field. Example, <input type= "text" name="name"> provides a text field.

The following is a list of all types of HTML <input> elements:

1. Text: It defines a single-line text input field.

Example:

```
<!doctype html>
<html>
  <head>
    <meta charset="utf-8">
    <meta  content="width=device-width,
name="viewport" initial-scale=1">
    <title> HTML </title>
  </head>
  <body>
    <main>
      <h1> HTML Form </h1>
      <form>
        <label>Enter first name</label><br>
        <input type="text" name="firstname"><br>
        <label>Enter last name</label><br>
        <input type="text" name="Lastname"><br>
      </form>
    </main>
  </body>
</html>
```

2. password: It defines a one-line field for entering a password

Example:

```
<!doctype html>
<html>
  <head>
    <meta charset="utf-8">
    <meta  content="width=device-width,
name="viewport" initial-scale=1">
    <title> HTML </title>
  </head>
  <body>
    <main>
      <h1> HTML Form </h1>
```

```
    <form>
      <form action="index.html">
        <label>Enter User name</label><br>
        <input type="text" name="firstname"><br>
        <label>Enter Password</label><br>
        <input type="Password"
name="password"><br>
        <br> <input type="submit"
value="submit">
      </form>
    </main>
  </body>
</html>
```

3. Submit: It defines a button to submit the form to the server.

Example:

```
<!doctype html>
<html>
  <head>
    <meta charset="utf-8">
    <meta  content="width=device-width,
name="viewport" initial-scale=1">
    <title> HTML </title>
  </head>
  <body>
    <main>
      <h1> HTML Form </h1>
      <form>
        <label>User id: </label>
        <input type="text" name="user-id"
value="user">
        <label>Password: </label>
        <input type="password" name="password"
value="pass"> <br> <br>
        <input type="submit" value="login">
    </form>
    </main>
  </body>
</html>
```

4. reset: It defines a reset button to reset all values in the form.

Example:

```
<!doctype html>
<html>
  <head>
    <meta charset="utf-8">
    <meta content="width=device-width,
name="viewport" initial-scale=1">
    <title> HTML </title>
  </head>
  <body>
    <main>
      <h1> HTML Form </h1>
      <form>
        <label> User id: </label>
          <input type="text" name="user-id"
value="user">
          <label>Password: </label>
          <input type="password" name="password"
value="pass"> <br> <br>
            <input type="reset" value="Reset">
      </form>
      </main>
  </body>
</html>
```

5. radio: It defines a radio button that allows you to select one option.

Example:

```
<!doctype html>
<html>
  <head>
    <meta charset="utf-8">
      <meta  content="width=device-width,
name="viewport" initial-scale=1">
    <title> HTML </title>
  </head>
  <body>
    <main>
```

```
    <h1> HTML Form </h1>
    <form>
       <p> Kindly Select your favorite color </p>
          <input type="radio" name="color"
value="red"> Red <br>
          <input type="radio" name="color"
value="blue"> blue <br>
          <input type="submit" value="submit">
       </form>
     </main>
   </body>
</html>
```

6. checkbox: It defines checkboxes that allow multiple form options to be selected.

Example:

```
<!doctype html>
<html>
  <head>
    <meta charset="utf-8">
      <meta  content="width=device-width,
name="viewport" initial-scale=1">
    <title> HTML </title>
  </head>
  <body>
    <main>
      <h1> HTML Form </h1>
      <form>
         <p> Kindly Select your favourite
programming language </p>
 <input type="text" name="name">
 <input type="checkbox" name="lang"
value="cricket"> HTML <br>
    <input type="checkbox"  name="lang"
value="baseball"> CSS <br>
      <input type="checkbox" name="lang"
value="badminton"> PHP <br>
         <input type="submit" value="submit">
```

```
      </form>
    </main>
  </body>
</html>
```

7. button: It defines a simple button that can be programmed to perform a task on an event.

Example:

```
<!doctype html>
<html>
  <head>
    <meta charset="utf-8">
    <meta  content="width=device-width,
name="viewport" initial-scale=1">
    <title> HTML </title>
  </head>
  <body>
    <main>
      <h1> HTML Form </h1>
      <form>
        <input type="button" value=" Click "
onclick="alert(' Now you are learning HTML')">
      </form>
    </main>
  </body>
</html>
```

8. file: It defines the selection of a file from the device storage.

Example:

```
<!doctype html>
<html>
  <head>
    <meta charset="utf-8">
     <meta content="width=device-width,
name="viewport" initial-scale=1">

    <title> HTML </title>
  </head>
```

```
<body>
  <main>
    <h1> HTML Form </h1>
    <form>
      <label>Select file to upload:</label>
      <input type="file" name="newfile">
      <input type="submit" value="submit">
    </form>
  </main>
</body>
</html>
```

9. image: It defines a graphic submit button.

Example:

```
<!doctype html>
<html>
  <head>
    <meta charset="utf-8">
    <meta   content="width=device-width,
name="viewport" initial-scale=1">
    <title> HTML </title>
  </head>
  <body>
    <main>
      <h1> HTML Form </h1>
      <form>
        <h3> Choose your image </h3>
        <input type="image" alt="Submit"
src="login.png"  width="100px">
      </form>
    </main>
  </body>
</html>
```

HTML5 added new types to the <input> element. The following is a list of HTML5 element types:

1. color: It defines an input field with a specific color.

Example:

```
<!doctype html>
<html>
```

```
   <head>
     <meta charset="utf-8">
      <meta content="width=device-width,
name="viewport" initial-scale=1">

    <title> HTML </title>
   </head>
   <body>
     <main>
       <h1> HTML Form </h1>
       <form>
           Pick your Favourite color: <br> <br>
           <input type="color"  value="#a52a2a">
s<br>
           <input type="color" value="#f5f5dc">
           </form>
     </main>
   </body>
</html>
```

2. Date: It defines an input field for selecting a date.

Example:

```
<!doctype html>
<html>
   <head>
     <meta charset="utf-8">
      <meta content="width=device-width,
name="viewport" initial-scale=1">

    <title> HTML </title>
   </head>
   <body>
     <main>
       <h1> HTML Form </h1>
       <form>
         <input type="date" name="date"> Add the
date <br>
         <label>
           Select date & time: <input
type="datetime-local" name="meetingdate"> <br>
         </label>
```

```
      </form>
   </main>
  </body>
</html>
```

3. DateTime-local: It defines an input field for entering a date without a time zone.

Example:

```
<!doctype html>
<html>
  <head>
    <meta charset="utf-8">
    <meta name="viewport" content="width=device-
width, initial-scale=1">
    <title> HTML </title>
  </head>
  <body>
    <main>
      <h1> HTML Form </h1>
      <form>
        <label>
          Select date & time: <input
type="datetime-local" name="meetingdate"> <br>
        </label>
          </form>
    </main>
  </body>
</html>
```

4. email: It defines an input field for entering an email address.

Example:

```
<!doctype html>
<html>
  <head>
    <meta charset="utf-8">
    <meta content="width=device-width,
name="viewport" initial-scale=1">
```

```
      <title> HTML </title>
   </head>
   <body>
     <main>
       <h1> HTML Form </h1>
       <form>
          <label> <b>Enter Email-addresses </b>
</label>
          <input type="email" name="email" >
          <input type="email"
name="email"  multiple>
        </form>
      </main>
   </body>
</html>
```

5. month: It defines a control with a month and year, without a time zone.

Example:

```
<!doctype html>
<html>
   <head>
     <meta charset="utf-8">
     <meta  content="width=device-width,
name="viewport" initial-scale=1">
     <title> HTML </title>
   </head>
   <body>
     <main>
       <h1> HTML Form </h1>
       <form>
         <label>Enter  Birthday year </label>
         <input type="month" name="newMonth">
           </form>
      </main>
   </body>
</html>
```

6. number: It defines an input field for entering a number.

Example:

```
<!doctype html>
<html>
  <head>
    <meta charset="utf-8">
    <meta  content="width=device-width,
name="viewport" initial-scale=1">
    <title> HTML </title>
  </head>
  <body>
    <main>
      <h1> HTML Form </h1>
      <form>
        <label> Enter your age: </label>
        <input type="number" name="num" min="50"
max="80">
      </form>
    </main>
  </body>
</html>
```

7. URL: It defines a field for entering a URL.

Example:

```
<!doctype html>
<html>
  <head>
    <meta charset="utf-8">
    <meta content="width=device-width,
name="viewport" initial-scale=1">


    <title> HTML </title>
  </head>
  <body>
    <main>
      <h1> HTML Form </h1>
      <form>
```

```
        <input type="url" name="website"
placeholder="http://google.com"><br>
        </form>
      </main>
    </body>
</html>
```

8. week: It defines a date input field with week and year, without time zone.

Example:

```
<!doctype html>
<html>
  <head>
    <meta charset="utf-8">
    <meta content="width=device-width,
name="viewport"  initial-scale=1">
    <title> HTML </title>
  </head>
  <body>
    <main>
      <h1> HTML Form </h1>
      <form>
        <label> <b> Select your  week of year:</b>
</label> <br>
          <input type="week" name="week">
        </form>
      </main>
    </body>
</html>
```

9. Search: It defines a one-line text field for entering a search string.

Example:

```
<!doctype html>
<html>
  <head>
    <meta charset="utf-8">
    <meta  content="width=device-width,
name="viewport" initial-scale=1">
```

```
    <title> HTML </title>
  </head>
  <body>
    <main>
      <h1> HTML Form </h1>
      <form>
        <label> <b>  Search word </b> </label>
<br>
        <input type="search" name="q">
      </form>
    </main>
  </body>
</html>
```

10. tel: It defines an input field for entering a telephone number.

Example:

```
<!doctype html>
<html>
  <head>
    <meta charset="utf-8">
    <metacontent="width=device-width,
name="viewport"  initial-scale=1">
    <title> HTML </title>
  </head>
  <body>
    <main>
      <h1> HTML Form </h1>
      <form>
        <input type="tel" name="telephone"
pattern="[0-9]{3}-[0-9]{3}-[0-9]{4}" required>
      </form>
    </main>
  </body>
</html>
```

HTML INPUT ATTRIBUTES

Here we describe the different attributes for the HTML <input> element.[7] There are various attributes of input. The list is given below:

- The value attribute: The meaning and use of the value depend on the element. The value attribute on an element sets the value of the element. Elements that accept a value include <input>, <button>, <option>, <data>, <li>, <meter>, <progress>, and <param>.

Example:

```
<!DOCTYPE html>
<html lang="en">
<head>
    <meta charset="UTF-8">
    <meta HTTP-equiv="X-UA-Compatible"
content="IE=edge">
    <meta name="viewport" content="width=device-
width, initial-scale=1.0">
    <title>Document</title>
</head>
<body>
    <form>
        <h2> HTML Input form attributes </h2>
        First name   <input type="text"
name="firstname" value="Alia"><br /><br />
        Last name   <input type="text"
name="Lastname" value="Grill"><br /><br />
        <label>Gender</label>  
          <label for="male"><input
type="radio" id="male" name="gender"
value="male" checked> Male</label>
          <label for="female"><input
type="radio" id="female" name="gender"
value="female"> Female</label>
          <label for="other"><input
type="radio" id="other" name="gender"
value="other"> Other</label><br /><br />
        <input type="submit" value="Submit">
        </form>
</body>
</html>
```

- The disabled attribute

Example:

```
<!DOCTYPE html>
<html lang="en">
<head>
    <meta charset="UTF-8">
    <meta HTTP-equiv="X-UA-Compatible"
content="IE=edge">
    <meta name="viewport" content="width=device-
width, initial-scale=1.0">
    <title>Document</title>
</head>
<body>
    <form>
        <h2> HTML Input form attributes </h2>
        First name   <input type="text"
name="firstname" value="Alia" disabled > <br />
        Last name   <input type="text"
name="Lastname" value="Grill"><br />
        <input type="submit" value="Submit">
    </form>
</body>
</html>
```

- The readonly attribute

Example:

```
<!DOCTYPE html>
<html lang="en">
<head>
    <meta charset="UTF-8">
    <meta HTTP-equiv="X-UA-Compatible"
content="IE=edge">
    <meta name="viewport" content="width=device-
width, initial-scale=1.0">
    <title>Document</title>
</head>
<body>
    <form>
```

```
        <h2> HTML Input form attributes </h2>
        <input type="text" id="fname"
name="fname" value="John" readonly> <br>
        Last name   <input type="text"
name="Lastname" value="Grill"><br />
        <input type="submit" value="Submit">
        </form>
</body>
</html>
```

- The max length and size attribute

Example:

```
<!DOCTYPE html>
<html lang="en">
<head>
    <meta charset="UTF-8">
    <meta HTTP-equiv="X-UA-Compatible"
content="IE=edge">
    <meta name="viewport" content="width=device-
width, initial-scale=1.0">
    <title>Document</title>
</head>
<body>
    <form>
        <h2> HTML Input form attributes </h2>
        First name   <input type="text"
size="30"  maxlength="4"
size="4"  name="firstname" value="Alia" > <br />
        Last name   <input type="text"
name="Lastname"  maxlength="4" size="4"
value="Grill"><br />
        <input type="submit" value="Submit">
        </form>
</body>
</html>
```

- The multiple attribute

Example:

```
<!DOCTYPE html>
<html lang="en">
<head>
    <meta charset="UTF-8">
    <meta HTTP-equiv="X-UA-Compatible"
content="IE=edge">
    <meta name="viewport" content="width=device-
width, initial-scale=1.0">
    <title>Document</title>
</head>
<body>
    <form>
        <h2> Add multiple images </h2>
        <input type="file" id="files"
name="files" multiple>
        <input type="submit" value="Submit">
    </form>
</body>
</html>
```

- The pattern attribute

Example:

```
<!DOCTYPE html>
<html lang="en">
<head>
    <meta charset="UTF-8">
    <meta HTTP-equiv="X-UA-Compatible"
content="IE=edge">
    <meta name="viewport" content="width=device-
width, initial-scale=1.0">
    <title>Document</title>
</head>
<body>
    <form>
        <h2> HTML Input form attributes </h2>
        <input type="text" id="name" name="name"
```

```
        pattern="[A-Za-z]{3}" >
    </form>
</body>
</html>
```

- The placeholder attribute

Example:

```
<!DOCTYPE html>
<html lang="en">
<head>
    <meta charset="UTF-8">
    <meta HTTP-equiv="X-UA-Compatible"
content="IE=edge">
    <meta name="viewport" content="width=device-
width, initial-scale=1.0">
    <title>Document</title>
</head>
<body>
    <form>
        <h2> HTML Input form attributes </h2>
        <input type="text" id="name" name="name"
placeholder="Name">
    </form>
</body>
</html>
```

- The required attribute

Example:

```
<html lang="en">
<head>
    <meta charset="UTF-8">
    <meta HTTP-equiv="X-UA-Compatible"
content="IE=edge">
    <meta name="viewport" content="width=device-
width, initial-scale=1.0">
    <title>Document</title>
</head>
<body>
```

```
<form>
    <h2> Add multiple images </h2>
    <input type="file" id="files"
name="files" required>
    <input type="submit" value="Submit">
    </form>
</body>
</html>
```

- The autofocus attribute

Example:

```
<html lang="en">
<head>
    <meta charset="UTF-8">
    <meta HTTP-equiv="X-UA-Compatible"
content="IE=edge">
    <meta name="viewport" content="width=device-
width, initial-scale=1.0">
    <title>Document</title>
</head>
<body>
    <form>
        <h2> Add multiple images </h2>
        <input type="file" id="files"
name="files" autofocus>
        <input type="submit" value="Submit">
        </form>
</body>
</html>
```

- The autocomplete attribute

Example:

```
<!DOCTYPE html>
<html lang="en">
<head>
    <meta charset="UTF-8">
    <meta HTTP-equiv="X-UA-Compatible"
content="IE=edge">
    <meta name="viewport" content="width=device-
width, initial-scale=1.0">
```

```
        <title>Document</title>
    </head>
    <body>
        <form>
            <h2> HTML Input form attributes </h2>
            <input type="text" id="name" name="name"
    placeholder="Name">
            <input type="email" id="email"
    name="email" autocomplete="off">
        </form>
    </body>
    </html>
```

CHAPTER SUMMARY

In this chapter, we discussed all the forms in the HTML. This chapter also contains all the necessary information related to the HTML tables. You can also refer to the given examples.

NOTES

1. HTML Forms – https://www.studytonight.com/cascading-style-sheet/css-forms, accessed on August 17, 2022.
2. HTTP Method – https://rapidapi.com/blog/api-glossary/get/, accessed on August 17, 2022.
3. HTML Input Control – https://www.tutorialspoint.com/html/html_forms.htm, accessed on August 17, 2022.
4. HTML Radio – https://www.educative.io/answers/radio-button-in-html, accessed on August 17, 2022.
5. HTML Buttons – https://www.tutorialspoint.com/html/html_forms.htm, accessed on August 17, 2022.
6. HTML Input Types – https://www.w3schools.com/html/html_form_input_types.asp, accessed on August 18, 2022.
7. HTML Input Attributes – https://www.w3schools.com/html/html_form_attributes.asp, accessed on August 18, 2022.

CSS

GETTING INTO THIS CHAPTER

➤ Introduction

➤ History of CSS

➤ Linking HTML with CSS files

➤ CSS Concepts in brief

In this chapter, we will learn Cascading Style Sheets (CSS), its fundamental concepts, versions, syntax, and how we can link our HTML page with CSS files. More concepts, like modules, selectors, ids, classes, borders, tables, forms, colors, etc., will also be discussed in the chapter.

So let's get started with CSS.

INTRODUCTION

A document is usually a text file created using tag language – HTML is the most common markup language, but you can merge it with other tag languages such as SVG or XML. It is presenting a document to a user means converting it into a form used by audience. The Browsers, like Firefox, Chrome, or Edge, are designed to deliver text by view.

CSS is a programming language that integrates all relevant information related to web page display.[1] It defines the style and format of a website or page, including layout, colors, margins, fonts, padding (space around each element), and more. Along with HTML and Javascript, CSS forms

DOI: 10.1201/9781003358077-8

the basis of how the Internet works. All three standards and specifications are maintained by the World Wide Web Consortium (W3C).

CSS can be used to create a basic text style – for example, to change the color and size of titles and links. It can be used to build a structure to convert a single column of text into a structure with a content area and a separate bar for related information. It can be used for effects such as animation.

HISTORY

CSS is highly regarded by Norwegian Håkon Wium Lie, who, back in 1994, wanted to make a standard style sheet for the World Wide Web.[2] The first site tried for CSS is the Arena web browser. Since its first creation, Lie has continued to co-produce versions of CSS1, CSS2, RFC 2318 with Tim Berners-Lee, and Robert Cailliau. In the first decade of existence (1994–2004), CSS, in all the clarity, became the standard website that has a significant impact on the look and feel of the global web as we know it today. CSS3 was released in 1999.

Web standards are the topics to Lie's heart. Since the introduction of CSS, he has appealed to major technology players like Microsoft and other web browsers to support the standard web whole and continue to improve.

CSS SYNTAX

Now move on to the original CSS.[3] The first thing we will do is make paragraph text a different color. So type or paste this into style file.css.

```
p {color: blue; }
```

This looks different from the code in HTML file because it is a different syntax. We will add a white area and cut it into code as follows:

```
p {
  color: blue;
}
```

Both of the above examples are exactly the same about browser. But developers often write CSS as the latest example to differentiate styles.

CSS is a rule-based language that defines rules by specifying groups of styles to be applied to specific objects or groups of objects on your web page. For example, you may decide that a major topic on your page is shown as a red flag. The following code shows a simple CSS rule.

```
p {
    color: red;
    font-size: 5em;
}
```

- For example, the CSS rule opens with a selector.

- Selects the HTML element that will style it. In this case, we style the first-level titles (<p>).

- Then we have a set of twisted pieces {}.

- Inside the instruments, there will be one or more announcements, which take the form of the goods and pairs of value. Specifies the location (color in the example above) before the colon, and specifies the value of the property after the colon (red for example).

- This example contains two declarations, one color and one font size. Each pair specifies the location of the element (s) we select (<p> in this case), and then the value we would like to give the structure.

CSS layouts have different valid values, depending on the specified format.[4] In our example, we have a color package, which can take on different color values. We also have a font size structure. This structure can take units of various sizes as a value.

The CSS style sheet will contain many such rules, written in sequence.

```
p {
    color: red;
    font-size: 5em;
}

h2 {
    color: black;
}
```

DIFFERENT TYPES OF CSS YOU CAN USE

We have three types of CSS[5]:

- CSS might appear in another external file.

- It may appear inside the top of a document or webpage.

- It may appear in the queue, next to the CSS text.

External Style Sheets contain CSS instructions, and these are special files and have a .css file extension. If an external style sheet is installed on any web page, the CSS file will control its sound and appearance.

A DIFFERENT VERSION OF CSS

CSS3 and CSS4 – These versions build in CSS2.1, adding new functionality and maintaining backward compatibility.[6] Some features are still being tested and may change in the future. Use this with caution, as it may cause problems with your site.

CSS2.1 (recommended) – This version has fixed many bugs and problems in CSS2 and is now the official recommended version of CSS.

CSS1 and CSS2 (no longer applicable) – These were the first two versions of CSS and are no longer updated or maintained.

STARTING WITH A SPECIFIC HTML

HTML and CSS are two methods of tags (code) with their own unique syntax. There is an important difference between the two. You can think of HTML as a page layout, while CSS gives HTML its own style.

```
HTML = structure
CSS = style
```

LINKING YOUR HTML AND CSS FILES

Before we can write CSS, we actually have to go back to our HTML. We need to write a new line to link the HTML file and CSS file together. So, open the HTML file and add the provided line "<link href =" style.css "rel =" stylesheet "type =" text / CSS "/>". Your file code looks like this:

```
<!DOCTYPE html>
<html>
```

```
<head>
  <title>This is page title.</title>
  <link  rel="stylesheet" type="text/CSS" href="style.
css" />
  </head>
  <body>
  <h1>This is a heading element</h1>
  <p>Hello world, this is a paragraph.</p>
  </body>
<html>
```

This line of code links a new CSS file to your HTML file. Let's split it: the href attribute specifies the link associated with the CSS file. We'll get to the links later, for now, just make sure the style.css file is in the same folder as index.html file. The rel attribute tells your browser that this is a style sheet. The attribute type tells the browser that this linked file should be translated as CSS syntax.

HOW CSS AND HTML WORK TOGETHER

CSS is only concerned with web page layout, while page content is defined using marker language such as HTML. The separation of style and content has various advantages, among them improved accessibility, and more control over web design.

CSS documents are used to define a web page style, then linked to an HTML document (or document in a different tag language) that contains the content and layout of the page. Setting the style directly to the HTML document is possible, but not recommended. CSS texts can be created in any text editor, such as Text Editor on Mac or Notepad for Windows, as well as many other free or paid options that you can download.

How to Apply Classes on Paragraph in HTML?

```
<html>
    <head> Title </head>
    <body>
    <! -- After creating the classes, you can apply
them to HTML elements: -->
    <p class="text">This is an example of a sentence
with regular font size</p></body>
    </html>
```

There are some things you need to look for when creating classes in CSS, such as the attributes you will add to the elements and the number of classes you want to create. If you plan this in advance, it will help you to edit the code easily.

Overall, you should also pay attention to these three factors:

- Specify your class – the name of the class should provide information about the attributes added to the feature. Therefore, it will be easier to understand. For example, if you want to add a class that will change the font size to 36, the best bet would be to name it a font-36.

- Make sure the class does only one thing – adding more than one attribute might make the class harder to use again. For example, you cannot use a class that contains two attributes – green text and 36 pixel font size if you only want green text without changing the font size.

- Organize your classes based on their characteristics – when you create classes, organize them based on their usage. For example, you can collect classes related to font size. This practice would help you in the long run.

CSS classes will help you style HTML elements quickly. Additionally, you can avoid duplicating the same code for each HTML object using the same style. Therefore, the amount of CSS code to be used decreases – making it more readable and easier to remove.

In another note, you can also use the ID selector to style HTML elements. However, it can only change one HTML object, and the class selector can create more than one object.

CSS COMMENTS

CSS comments are not visible in the browser but may be helpful in writing your source code.[7] Comments are also used to explain the code and can be helpful if you edit the source code later. Comments ignored by browsers. CSS comments are embedded within the <style> element, and begin with / / and end with * /:

Example:

```
/* This is a one-line comment   */
p {
```

```
    color: red;
}
```

You can add comments where you want to code:

Example:

```
p {
    color: red;    /* * Set text color in red  */
}


/* This
many lines
comment

*/

p {
    color: red;
}
```

CSS Colors

Here is a table of basic color names that have been in CSS since CSS1. Try clicking a value. This will open the color in the online editor of Quick to see what it looks like. There is a link to the color checker where you can get another color preview.

Color Names

Here is the full list of CSS color labels as specified in CSS3. These are based on the X-11 color set. The basic colors above are included in this chart. Try clicking a value. This will open the color in the online editor of Quick to see what it looks like. There is a link to the color checker where you can get another color preview.

How to Use These Colors

Each color can be represented in various different ways. For example, blue can be represented as # 0000ff, # 00f, RGB (0, 0, 255), and other ways. It does not matter which one you choose as long as it is a valid color. You can apply any of the colors to a website or blog by using the appropriate CSS code.

- To set the background color, use the background color.

- To set text color, use color.

- To set a border color, use the border color.

CSS SELECTORS

CSS selector for matching features on a web page.[8] The style rules connected with that selector will apply to items such as the pattern. Choices are one of the most important CSS features as they allow you to direct certain elements to your web page in a variety of ways to style them.

A few types of selectors are available in CSS, let's take a closer look.

Universal Selector

It is indicated by a star (*), corresponds to each part of the page. The universal selector may be removed if other conditions are present in the feature. This filter is often used to remove automatic genes and pads from elements for quick testing.

Let's try the following example to understand how it basically works:

```
*  {
    margin: 0;
    padding: 0;
}
```

The style rules within the selector * will apply to everything in the document.

Element Type Selectors

It is the same as every element in a document and the name of the corresponding element type. Let's try an example to see how it really works.

```
p {
    color: blue;
}
```

Id Selector

The id selector is used to describe style rules for one or more items. The id selector is defined by a hash (#) symbol that is immediately followed by the id value.

Example:

```
#text{
    color: red;
}
```

This style rule gives the text the object in red, its id identifier being set as default.

Class Selectors

It is used to select any HTML component with a class attribute. All features with that class will be formatted according to a defined rule. The class selector is defined by an intermediate symbol (.). That is immediately followed by a class value.

Example:

```
.green {
    color: blue;
}
```

Descendant Selectors

You can use these options if you need to select an interest-bearing element of another element, for example, if you want to identify only those anchors contained in the random list, rather than directing all anchor elements. Let's see an example on how it works.

```
ul.menu li a {
    text-decoration: none;
}
h1 em {
    color: green;
}
```

The style rules within the selector ul.menu li a apply only to those elements <a> contained within the <ul> element that has a class .menu, and that does not affect other links within the document. Similarly, style rules within the h1 em selector will only apply to those elements of <em> content contained within the element of <h1> and which do not affect other elements of <em>.

Child Selectors

The child selector is used to select only those specific child items for a particular feature. The children's selector is made up of two or more selectors that are separated by a larger symbol (>). You can use this selector, for example, to select the first level of list items within a nested list with more than one level. Let's look at an example on how it works.

```
ul > li {
    list-style: circle;
}
ul > li ol {
    list-style: none;
}
```

The style rule inside the selector, such as ul > li applied to only those <li> elements that direct children of the <ul> elements, has no effect on other list elements.

Adjacent Sibling Selectors

Adjacent sibling selectors are used to select its sibling elements (i.e., elements at the same level). This selector has a syntax such as: E1 + E2, where E2 is the target selector.

The h1 + p selector in the following example will select <p> elements only if the <h1> and <p> elements share the same parent in the document tree and <h1> precedes the <p> section immediately. This means that only those sections that come immediately after each <h1> title will have corresponding style rules. Let's see an example on how this option really works.

```
h1 + p {
    color: blue;
    font-size: 18px;
}
```

```
ul.text + p {
    color: black;
    font-size: 30px;
}
```

Sibling Selector

The standard sibling selector is similar to the nearest sibling selector (E1 + E2), but less powerful. The standard sibling selector is made up of two simple picks separated by a tilde (~) character. It can be written as follows: E1 ~ E2, where E2 is the purpose of the selector.

The h1 ~ p selector in the example below will select all the <p> features preceded by the <h1> section, where all the features share the same parent in the document tree.

```
h1 ~ p {
    color: blue;
    font-size: 18px;
}
ul.task ~ p {
    color: #f0f;
    text-indent: 30px;
}
```

Grouping Selectors

Usually, a few selectors on a style sheet share declarations of the same style rules. You can group them with a comma-separated list to narrow the code to your style sheet. It also prevents others from repeating the same style rules over and over again.

Let's take a look.

```
h1 {
    font-size: 36px;
    font-weight: normal;
}
h2 {
    font-size: 28px;
    font-weight: normal;
}
h3 {
    font-size: 22px;
    font-weight: normal;
}
```

SOME OTHER CONCEPTS OF CSS

There are various properties you can use to design your page using CSS listed below:

- CSS Syntax

- CSS Selectors

- CSS Comments

We have already discussed previously all the above-listed properties.

- CSS Colors

The color properties are specified using color names, or RGB, HEX, HSL, RGBA, and HSLA values. For example, #ff0000, RGB(0, 0, 0, 0.1), HSL(240 100% 50%), etc.

- CSS Backgrounds

The background properties are used to add background effects for elements. There are various other properties of background such as background-color, background-image, background-repeat, background-attachment, background-position, etc.

- CSS Borders: The border properties specify the style, width, and color of an element's border. The following values are allowed such as, dotted, dashed, solid, double, groove, ridge, inset, outset, none, and hidden.

- CSS Margins: CSS margins are used to create space around elements, without any defined parameters. There are features for setting the margin for each element of the element such as top, bottom, right, and left. CSS has features that specify a margin for each element of the element for margin-top, margin-bottom, margin-right, and margin-left.

- CSS Padding: CSS padding is used to generate space near element content, within any defined parameters. There are pad setup properties on each side of the element, such as top, bottom, right, and left. CSS has paddling specifications for each element of the element: padding-top, padding-bottom, padding-right, and padding-left.

- CSS Fonts: CSS Fonts defines font-related properties and how font resources are loaded. It also defines the style of a font, such as its family, size and weight, line height. There are various properties of font such as font, font-family, font-size, font-size-adjust, font-stretch, font-style, font-variant, etc.

- CSS Lists: The List specifies the listing of the contents or items in a particular manner which helps to make a clean webpage. The list can be categorized into two types such as Unordered List and Ordered List.

- CSS Tables: The table is used to apply various style elements to HTML table elements to organize data in rows and columns, or possibly in a more complex format. This feature is used to set the algorithm used to edit <table> cells, rows, and columns.

- CSS Display: The display property determines how an element looks. It is also a part of the presentation of code as it has a significant impact on layouts. The display property has different values such as inline, inline-block, block, grid, flex, none, inline-grid, and more, which all influence the layout and presentation of an element on the web page.

- CSS Position: The position property defines the type of positioning method used for an element. There are five different position values such as static, relative, fixed, absolute, and sticky.

- CSS Forms: Forms are a part of any website. It is a way to take user information and process requests. To add a form to a web page, we need to add a <form> element. All input fields and form controls should be wrapped in a <form> element.

- CSS Transitions: It allows changing property values smoothly, within a given duration. Here we have the following properties such as transition, transition-delay, transition-duration, transition-property, and transition-timing-function.

- CSS Animations: An animation lets an element change from one style to another. It has properties such as @keyframes, animation-name, animation-duration, animation-delay, animation-iteration-count, animation-direction, animation-timing-function, animation-fill-mode, animation.

- CSS Flexbox: The Flexbox layout allows you to easily format HTML. Flexbox makes it easy to direct objects horizontally and horizontally using lines and columns. Flexbox is a layout for arranging objects in rows or columns. The flex container properties are flex-direction, flex-wrap, flex-flow, justify-content, align-items, and align-content.

- CSS Grid: The Grid offers a grid-based layout system, with rows and columns, making it easier to design pages without having to use floats and positioning.

CHAPTER SUMMARY

Here we have discussed all the basic concepts of CSS that everyone can use to make their pages attractive. So an important thing for working with CSS is to just only practice. Once you start practicing it, you will get to the point easily.

NOTES

1. CSS Introduction – https://en.wikipedia.org/wiki/CSS, accessed on August 18, 2022.
2. CSS Introduction – https://www.w3.org/Style/CSS20/history.html, accessed on August 18, 2022.
3. CSS Syntax – https://www.w3.org/Style/LieBos2e/enter/Overview.en.html, accessed on August 18, 2022.
4. HTML Layout – http://web.simmons.edu/~grovesd/comm244/notes/week3/css-colors, accessed on August 18, 2022.
5. CSS Types – https://www.hostinger.in/tutorials/difference-between-inline-external-and-internal-css, accessed on August 18, 2022.
6. CSS Version – https://www.codingninjas.com/blog/2021/01/07/difference-between-css-css2-css3/, accessed on August 18, 2022.
7. CSS Comments – https://www.w3schools.com/css/css_comments.asp, accessed on August 18, 2022.
8. CSS Selector – https://developer.mozilla.org/en-US/docs/Learn/CSS/Building_blocks/Selectors/Type_Class_and_ID_Selectors, accessed on August 18, 2022.

Appraisal

This book represents the structure and content of HTML5. The book might be the same as the other but it is an all-new concept. Basically, as compared to the others version such as HTML4, this edition focuses more on HTML5 that represents a return to the markup past. However, we get some information from the previous version because we also focus on the previous elements that not only focus on the future but also present all the elements supported in browsers today. With the help of this book, we want to provide the reference you need in learning their syntax. However, in the case of web documents, the markup is in the form of traditional Hypertext Markup Language (HTML) and its Extensible Markup Language (XML). The XML-focused variant, XHTML, is a bit more obvious. These are not very behind-the-scenes markup languages that are used to inform web browsers about the structure of a page and some can argue presentation too.

Since HTML was introduced in 1991, HTML (and later its XML-based cousin, XHTML) has gone through many changes. The first versions of HTML were used to compile the earliest websites that lacked a precise definition. Then Internet Engineering Task Force (IETF) began to standardize the language. In 1995, the first released HTML standard in the form of HTML 2.0.

HTML is a markup language for creating web pages. Elements that are in the form of tags such as <em> and </em> are inserted into text documents to indicate to browsers how to render pages. Many of the elements that HTML5 adds that can be used immediately are semantic in nature. In this sense, HTML5 continues the appropriate goal of separating structure from style.

However, HTML5 is not only about markup; it is also about metadata, media, Web applications, APIs, and more.

DOI: 10.1201/9781003358077-9

HTML FEATURES

- HTML is the commonly used language for writing web pages.

- It is an easy to understand and editable language.

- You can do effective presentations that can be created using all its formatting tags.

- It provides a more flexible way to design web pages along with text.

- You can also add links to web pages so that readers can browse the information that interests them.

- HTML documents run on all platforms such as Macintosh, Windows, Linux, etc.

- More topics like graphics, videos, and sounds can also be added to the website to give your website an extra attractive look.

CAREER

HTML developers or programmers should have a bachelor's degree in computer science. There are many platforms available for HTML developers to help them improve their HTML skills. With the help of HTML, anyone can create their own websites and/or websites for different suppliers.

Since HTML is mainly used with other scripting languages, the scope of HTML always remains in the top organization and will be used in any web development such as web pages and web applications, although it is useful for creating custom applications or web pages. HTML can be used in multiple languages, and employers offer a good salary to web developers or HTML developers. HTML gives you customized features with less effort. A career in HTML is growing fast and learns it for creating your own websites as well.

Web development has two main parts namely Frontend and Backend. Frontend development is also called client-side web development. In this book, we have discussed frontend development in detail. This is mainly about creating websites or web applications for the client using HTML, CSS, and JavaScript. Anything that appears on the client side is something that users can interact with.

Frontend development is a constantly evolving field. Tools and techniques are constantly changing. A developer must always be ready to learn new skills because the market is very volatile. With every new library or framework that comes out, the developer has to constantly improve. Awareness of how the market is evolving is also important.

To become a frontend developer, one must learn how to architect and develop websites and applications using web technologies. These technologies run on an open web platform. They can also act as compilation input for non-web platforms such as React Native. Anyone entering the field of web development must learn HTML, CSS, and JavaScript. These three technologies are considered core.

How to Get a Job as Web Developer?

HTML is mainly required for frontend developers, full-stack developers, and UI/UX designers. It doesn't take long to learn HTML. Most new programmers can learn the basics of HTML in two to three weeks. However, daily practice is necessary to master the language and understand its full potential.

You should expect it to take at least a year to prepare for a "professional" job as a web developer. However, your learning never ends. HTML is still being updated today. There are hundreds of brands and advanced attributes to learn about.

If you want to master HTML, you should learn some topics of HTML such as –

- HTML structured

- HTML headings (<h1>, <h2>... <h6>)

- The <div> tag

- Presenting text using <p> and <span>

- Styling text using <style> and CSS

- Ordered and unordered lists (<ol> and <ul>)

- Adding image files (<img>)

- Table rows, columns, borders, head, body, and footer

- Form design and data collection

- Types of form questions like radio buttons, text boxes, and checkboxes

- CSS style rule

Index

Printed in the United States
by Baker & Taylor Publisher Services